Eigth Edition : 1995
(4,000 Copies)

Printed in recognition of the meritorious services rendered by
the Divine Life Society of South Africa, Durban

ISBN 81-7052-040-1

Published by Swami Krishnananda for The Divine Life Society,
Shivanandanagar, and printed by him at the Yoga-Vedanta Forest
Academy Press, P.O. Shivanandanagar, Distt. Tehri-Garhwal,
U.P., Himalayas, India

OM

Dedicated to

The Citizens of Tomorrow,

The Future Hope of the World

OM

SRI SWAMI SIVANANDA

PUBLISHERS' NOTE

The child is the father of man. It is often the first ideas which strike the mind of a child, and the nature of the impressions and thought-waves coming in contact with the tender intellect for the first time, that make up and contribute to the being of the later man. It was the perfect all-round training that Shivaji received from his mother, since his childhood, that moulded him into a jewel among Indian heroes.

It is said that you cannot begin too early in training the individual. Also education without the true religion is a mere husk, the dead bare bones of culture. Moreover, the child-mind learns more from examples than from naked truth.

Bearing all these points in vision, Sri Swamiji felt the absolute need for such a book for little children, as would help them to grasp the truths of ethical and spiritual culture in an easy manner. Himself being a firm believer in the truth that childhood is the foundation of the larger nations of the world, Swamiji has produced an excellent marvel to the young students of lower secondary and elementary schools in particular.

This book contains lessons on practically all that a child has to understand in the beginning of his studies in life-lessons on divine truths, saints, sages, devotees, epics, Puranas, health, character, morality, general knowledge, Bhakti, Yoga, Sadhana, etc.

We are sure that this wonderful guide-light to the real regeneration of education and culture of young boys and girls would find a necessary place in the curriculum of studies in all schools.

—THE DIVINE LIFE SOCIETY

PRAYER

ॐ गजाननं भूतगणादिसेवितं कपित्थजम्बूफलसारभक्षणम्।
उमासुतं शोकविनाशकारकं नमामि विघ्नेश्वरपादपङ्कजम् ॥

I worship the lotus feet of Ganesha, the son of Uma, the destroyer of all sorrows, who is served by the host of Devas and Bhutas and who takes the essence of Kapittha and Jambu fruits (resembling Bilva fruit).

गुरुर्ब्रह्मा गुरुर्विष्णुर्गुरुर्देवो महेश्वरः।
गुरुः साक्षात् परं ब्रह्म तस्मै श्रीगुरवे नमः॥

I bow to that Sri Guru who himself is Brahma, Vishnu and Mahesvara, and who is in reality the Supreme Para Brahman.

शान्ताकारं भुजगशयनं पद्मनाभं सुरेशं
विश्वाधारं गगनसदृशं मेघवर्णं शुभाङ्गम् ।
लक्ष्मीकान्तं कमलनयनं योगिभिर्ध्यानगम्यं
वन्दे विष्णुं भवभयहरं सर्वलोकैकनाथम् ॥

I bow to that Lord Vishnu whose form is Peace, who is sleeping on the bed of snake, who has lotus in the navel, who is God of gods, who is the support for this world, who is like ether, whose colour is like cloud, whose limbs are beautiful, who is the husband of Goddess Lakshmi, whose eyes are like lotus, who is obtained by Yogins in meditation, who destroys the fear of Samsara, and who is the one Lord of all the worlds.

VOICE OF THE HIMALAYAS

1. The cause of death is birth.
2. The cause of pain is pleasure.
3. Righteousness forms the bedrock of all religions.
4. Righteousness is the divine path.
5. Bliss is for him who is righteous.
6. Desire is poverty.
7. Meditation is a positive vital dynamic process. It transforms man into Divinity.
8. Be good. Do good. Serve, love, give, purify, meditate, realise. This is the religion of Siva. This is the religion of the members of the Divine Life Society.
9. Be kind. Be compassionate. Be honest. Be sincere. Be truthful. Be bold. Be pure. Be wise. Be virtuous. Enquire: 'Who am I?' Know thy Self and be free. This is the summary of the teachings of Siva.
10. Dedicate your entire life to the Lord. He will surely look after you in every respect and you will have no more worries.
11. Divine Life is a life of love, wisdom and light.
12. Awake, O aspirant! Do vigorous Sadhana. Burn all impurities. Attain illumination through meditation.

GURU BHAKTI

यस्य देवे परा भक्तिर्यथा देवे तथा गुरौ ।
तस्यैते कथिता ह्यर्थाः प्रकाशन्ते महात्मनः ॥

"Spiritual truths will stand revealed only unto him who has great devotion to God and has as great a devotion to his preceptor as he has to God," declares the Upanishad. The Reality or God that is beyond the mind and senses, reason and intellection, can hardly be understood by man by reading books or indulging in intellectual gymnastics even for a hundred lives; the Reality will even then have such significance to him as the characters of the Chinese alphabets to an illiterate South African aboriginal.

On the other hand a word from the master's lips, a touch of his divine hand, a thought from his master-mind, would be enough to enlighten the aspirant's intellect, to bestow upon him an intuitive realisation of the Reality or God, if only the aspirant had qualified himself for a spiritual communion with the preceptor. How is he to qualify himself? Says the Lord Krishna:

तद्विद्धि प्रणिपातेन परिप्रश्नेन सेवया ।
उपदेक्ष्यन्ति ते ज्ञानं ज्ञानिनस्तत्त्वदर्शिनः ॥

"Know That by prostrating yourself before, serving, and enquiring of, the Great Sages of Self-realisation. They will enlighten you."

A shining illustration of this grand truth we have in Sri Trotaka, one of the four great disciples of Sri Sankaracharya, who was more intent upon serving the illustrious master than on studying the Scriptures; through a mere Sankalpa Sri Sankara bestowed the highest knowledge upon Trotaka who gained all knowledge of the Shastras by mere personal service of the Guru.

Therefore it is that a sincere Sadhaka firmly believes:

ध्यानमूलं गुरोमूर्तिः पूजामूलं गुरोः पदम् ।
मन्त्रमूलं गुरोर्वाक्यं मोक्षमूलं गुरोः कृपा ॥

The Guru's Form Itself is fit to be meditated upon; the Guru's Feet are the object of the Sadhaka's worship; the Guru's words are gospel-truths; and the Guru's Grace is the bestower of Immortality.

CONTENTS

Chapter One

DIVINE WORSHIP

Chapter Two

SAGES AND SAINTS

Chapter Three

INDIAN HEROES AND HEROINES

Chapter Four

EPICS AND PURANAS

Chapter Five

HEALTH AND BRAHMACHARYA

Chapter Six

MORAL LESSONS

Chapter Seven

SPIRITUAL INSTRUCTIONS

Chapter Eight

MORAL STORIES

Chapter Nine

GENERAL KNOWLEDGE

Chapter Ten

SIVANANDA'S LETTERS

Chapter Eleven

CHILDREN'S SONGS

Chapter Twelve

MAXIMS

Chapter Thirteen

STORIES

DIVINE LIFE FOR CHILDREN

Chapter One

DIVINE WORSHIP

GLORY TO GOD

God created you, your brother, sister, father, mother, friend and your relatives. He created the sun, moon and the stars. He created the animals and the birds. He created the mountains, rivers and trees. He created this whole world.

He dwells in your heart. He is everywhere. He is all-pervading. He is all-knowing. He is all-powerful. He is all-merciful. He is all-loving. He is all-blissful. Your body is the moving temple of God. Keep the body pure, strong and healthy.

Pray to Him daily. He will give you everything.

GOD IS LOVE

God is Love. God is Truth. God is Peace. God is Bliss. God is Light. God is Power. God is Knowledge. Realise Him and be free.

Do Kirtan daily morning and night. Pray daily. Offer flowers to Him. Prostrate before Him. Offer sweetmeats to Him and then eat. Place light before Him. Burn camphor before Him. Do Arati. Put garland on Him.

Keep a picture of God in your room. Worship Him daily. All your desires will be fulfilled.

MORNING PRAYER TO GOD

O Lord of this world! Prostrations unto Thee! Thou art my Guru, real Mother, real Friend and real Guide. Protect me. I am Thine. All is Thine. Thy Will be done.

O Adorable God! Salutations unto Thee. Give me pure intellect. Make me pure. Give me light, strength, health and long life. Make me a good Brahmachari.

O Almighty Lord! Remove all my evil qualities. Make me virtuous. Make me a patriot. Let me love my mother-country.

NIGHT PRAYER TO GOD

O Sweet God! Forgive my sins and wrong actions. I thank You for all your gifts. You are very kind to me. Let me remember You always.

Make me dutiful. Give me success in my examination. Make me a good, brilliant boy. (Make me a good, brilliant girl.) Adorations unto Thee.

Give me good memory. Let me love all. Let me serve all. Let me see You in all. Make me prosperous. Protect me, my father, mother, grandfather, grandmother, brothers and sisters. Glory unto Thee!

WEEK-DAYS' WORSHIP

Worship Lord Surya on Sundays. Repeat Om Mitraya Namah, Om Suryaya Namah, Om Adityaya Namah. Lord Surya will give you good health and vigour and good eyesight.

Worship Lord Siva on Mondays. Worship Devi on Tuesdays and Fridays. Worship Guru on Thursdays. Worship Hanuman on Saturdays.

You will get plenty, peace, prosperity and success!

Lord Brahma is the creator of this world. Sarasvati, Goddess of learning, is His Sakti or energy or wife. Lord Vishnu is the preserver of this world. Goddess Lakshmi is His Sakti, energy or wife. She is the Goddess of wealth. Lord Siva is the destroyer of this world. Uma or Parvati is His Sakti, energy or wife. Lord Ganesha is His eldest son. Lord Subrahmanya is His second son!

Lord Ganesha removes all obstacles. Lord Subrahmanya gives all success and strength. Worship them with faith and devotion. You will get Bhakti, Bhukti and Mukti.

GOD LOVES YOU

God loves you. He gives you many good things. He gives you food to eat and clothes to wear. He has given you ears to hear, eyes to see, a nose to smell, tongue to taste, hands to feel and work and legs to walk.

You cannot see God with your fleshy eyes but He sees you. He takes care of you. He knows all that you do.

He is very kind to you. Love Him. Praise Him. Sing His name and glory. Pray to Him to keep you away from all sins. He will be pleased with you. He will bless you.

MOTHER GAYATRI

Gayatri is the blessed Mother of the Vedas. She is the Mother for your mother also. She is a Devi.

Repeat Gayatri daily morning, noon and evening if

you wear holy thread. Do Sandhya-Vandana regularly. Offer Arghya to sun.

"Om Bhur Bhuvah Svah Tat Savitur Varenyam Bhargo Devasya Dheemahi Dhiyo Yo Nah Prachodayat."

"Let us meditate on Ishvara and His glory, who has created this Universe, who is fit to be worshipped, who is the remover of all sins and ignorance. May He enlighten our intellect."

May Mother Gayatri bless you with health, long life and prosperity.

BEAUTY IS GOD

O David! Look at the rose! How beautiful it is! What a fine fragrance it has! You love it. You pluck it and smell it. Can a scientist produce a rose? You can make a paper-flower which may look beautiful but it has no sweet smell.

The rose soon fades and loses its beauty and fragrance. You throw it away. It is perishable. Its beauty lasts for a few minutes.

Who has created the beautiful flower? This Creator is God. He is Beauty of beauties. He is everlasting Beauty. Attain Him. You also will possess eternal beauty. Beauty is God. Always discriminate between the real and the unreal.

ONLY ONE GOD

There is only one God. But names and aspects are endless. Call Him by any name and worship Him in any aspect that pleases you. You are sure to see Him and get His grace and blessings.

Brahma, Vishnu and Siva are the three Forms of the one God of the Hindus. Allah is the God of Muslims. Jehovah is the God of the Jews. The Father in Heaven is the God of Christians. Ahura Mazda is the God of the Zoroastrians.

Purity, charity, control of the senses, penance, truthfulness, renunciation, compassion to all beings, courage, fortitude, absence of hatred and pride will help you to attain God.

GOD IS THE CENTRE

God is the Aim of all religions. Every religion points out the way to attain God. God is the central topic of every religion.

Do not fight with your Christian friends. Do not fight with your Muslim friends or Parsee friends. Their religions also lead them to God just as your religion does. You can reach the same destination by travelling through any of the paths leading to it. "All roads lead to God." Bear this in mind.

Chapter Two

SAGES AND SAINTS

SRI VASISHTHA MAHARSHI

Vasishtha is the most powerful of Brahma's sons. He was born from Brahma's Prana or life itself. He was a born Brahma-Jnani. No Rishi or sage is equal to Vasishtha in spiritual energy. He is God Himself. His strength is indescribable.

Vishvamitra, another Rishi wanted to conquer Vasishtha. Vishvamitra did many thousand-years' Tapas and got all divine weapons. Then he fought with Vasishtha. Vasishtha consumed all those weapons by mere Will. Vishvamitra could not do anything. Vishvamitra's army and his hundred sons were destroyed by Vasishtha's Will-power. Glory to Vasishtha's Will-power. Glory to Vasishtha.

Vasishtha is an ideal Maharshi. Worship him daily. All his teachings are found in the Yoga-Vasishtha.

SRI VEDAVYASA

There was a great sage called Parasara. He had a powerful son called Dvaipayana through Sri Satyavati Devi. She was a fisher-woman. But the son was a famous Rishi. He wrote many books. He edited the four Vedas,

Rik, Yajus, Sama and the Atharva. He compiled the Vedas. Therefore he was called Vedavyasa.

He wrote the great epic, Mahabharata. It contains the whole wisdom of the world. He wrote the eighteen Puranas. He wrote the Vedanta Sutras. He was a great Jnani.

He had a son called Suka. He was also a very powerful Rishi. He could see God everywhere.

Worship Vyasa as your Guru. He will bless you. Become a saint like Suka.

LORD BUDDHA

There was once a Shakya king called Shuddhodana. He had a son called Siddhartha. Siddhartha was very softhearted from the very beginning. He was very kind to all beings. One day he saw a corpse being carried. He came to know that he too would die one day in the same manner. Another time he saw a hawk eating a dove mercilessly. He saw many pitiable incidents like this.

Siddhartha grew restless and impatient when he saw the miseries of the world. He grew dispassionate. One night he stole from his bedroom leaving his family and the kingdom. He sat under a Bodhi-tree for austere practices. He got enlightenment and was called thereafter, the "Buddha".

He preached to the world the law of Ahimsa or noninjury. Possess the heart of Buddha. Buddha is one of the most conspicuous figures in the history of the world.

SRI SANKARACHARYA

Sri Sankaracharya is the greatest philosopher of

India. He is the Avatara of Lord Siva. He took Sannyasa at a very early age. He was highly intellectual. He knew the real nature of God. He gave new life to the dying Hinduism, which was under the influence of Buddhistic doctrines. He was the upholder of Advaita Philosophy.

He wrote commentaries on the Upanishads, Brahmasutras and the Bhagavadgita. Before his sixteenth year he had mastered all knowledge. He defeated all Pundits and scholars in argument. He wrote the Vivekachudamani, a very inspiring Vedantic text for beginners.

Sri Sankara wrote about 108 works. He is one of the greatest sages India has ever produced. He passed away at the age of 32. He elevated the whole of India in this short period. Glory to Sankara!

SRI VIDYARANYA MUNI

Sri Vidyaranya Swami is otherwise known as Madhavacharya. He was next to Sankara in Advaitic knowledge. He wrote the famous commentaries on the four Vedas. He wrote the Panchadasi, Anubhutiprakasha, Jivanmuktiviveka, etc. He was a great Tapasvin. He won the favour of Gayatri Devi. Gayatri Devi showered golden rain near Hampi in South India.

He founded the famous Vijayanagara Empire through the two brothers, Hukka and Bukka. Hence, he is regarded as a nation-builder. He saved the people from the tyranny of the rule of Mohammed-bin-Tughlak and his successors.

Vidyaranya was an ideal sage. Become like Vidyaranya in Tapas, righteousness, wisdom and sacrifice.

GURU NANAK

Guru Nanak was the first of the Sikh Gurus. He was born at Talwandi in 1469. This place is now called Nankana Sahib. He is the founder of the Sikh religion. He was religious-minded even when he was a boy.

His father Kaloo wanted to make Nanak a shop-keeper like him. Nanak gave up his studies and spent his time in the company of holy men.

He composed many songs in praise of God. These are collected in a book called the Granth Sahib. The Sikhs worship this book. He tried to unite the Hindus and the Muslims. He died in 1539, at the age of seventy.

LORD JESUS

Lord Jesus is the founder of the religion known as Christianity. He was a great Yogi. He was a great prophet or messenger of God. He did many miracles. He served the poor and the lepers. Virgin Mary was his mother.

His wonderful message is known as 'The Sermon on the Mount'. He had twelve devout disciples who preached to people the way of God as taught by Jesus.

STUDY THE LIVES OF SAINTS

Study of the lives of saints will elevate you. You will become a very good boy. You will develop virtues. You will see God face to face.

Tuka Ram, Jnana Dev, Ekanath, Nama Dev and Rama Das were the great saints from Maharashtra. Lord Gouranga was a great saint from Bengal.

Mira Bai and Sakku Bai were great lady-saints. Guru

Nanak, Kabir, Narsi Mehta, Sur Das, Tulsi Das were also great saints.

Saint Joseph, Saint Francis, Saint Patrick were great Christian saints.

May these Saints bless you all!

GOSWAMI TULASIDAS

Goswami Tulasidas was a great devotee of Lord Rama. He had direct Darshana of Lord Rama through intense devotion. He was very much attached to his wife. His wife became his Guru.

He was born in 1589 in Rajpur in the district of Banda in the Uttar Pradesh. He was a Brahmin by birth. He was born with all the thirty-two teeth intact. He did not cry at the time of his birth.

The great Ramayana of Goswami Tulasidas in Hindi is a masterpiece. This work is very popular and is studied widely in North India.

Study the Ramayana daily. Get by heart some Chopais and sing.

AJAMILA

Ajamila was a pious Brahmin. He daily worshipped God. He was very kind towards all. He was very regular in his duties. He observed fast on Ekadasi. He was an ideal man. He was a great devotee of Lord Narayana. He was very regular in his prayer.

One day he went to the forest. There he met a beautiful lady. He fell in love with her. He married her. From that day he left his worship and prayer. He was very much attached to his wife. Eight sons were born to him. He became a Nastika.

At the time of death the messengers of Yama appeared before him. He was frightened. He cried aloud. He called his youngest son Narayana to come for help. At once the messengers of Vishnu came to the spot and drove Yama's messengers and took Ajamila to Vaikuntha.

Repeat always the names of Lord Narayana. Ajamila reached the abode of bliss by unintentional repetition of Hari's Name. How much more will be the effect of repeating His Names with faith and devotion!

PURANDAR DAS

There was once a Brahmin in Purandargarh. He was a very greedy miser. Lord Krishna wanted to test his greed. He came as a beggar to the Brahmin and asked for alms. The Brahmin refused to give anything and asked him to come the next day. The beggar came the next day also. The Brahmin asked him to come still another day. The beggar persisted everyday like this for months together.

The Brahmin at last grew angry and threw a pie on the beggar's face. The beggar left it and went behind the Brahmin's house. The beggar got as alms the nose-ring from the Brahmin's wife. The beggar sold the ornament to the same Brahmin for money and went away.

The Brahmin grew angry at his wife. He asked her: "Where is your ornament?" She said she would bring it from inside. She wanted to take poison in fear. But she found the ornament there. She gave it to her husband.

He was wonder-struck. He became a saint and a devotee from that day.

Chapter Three

INDIAN HEROES AND HEROINES

RAMA AND KRISHNA

Lord Krishna is the great Yogesvara. Rama and Krishna are one. Rama was born in Ayodhya, Krishna was born in Mathura. Sita was the wife of Rama. Radha was the wife of Krishna.

Rama had bow in His hand. Krishna had flute and discus in His hand. Rama killed Ravana. Krishna killed Kamsa and many other eveil-doers.

Rama is Maryada-Purushottama. Krishna is Lila-Purushottama. Rama's brother is Lakshmana. Krishna's brother is Balarama. Sing Sita Ram and Radhe Shyam.

SRI HANUMAN

Sri Hanuman is the son of wind-god or Vayu Bhagavan. His mother is Anjana Devi. He is the most devoted servant and messenger of Lord Rama. He is a mighty hero. He is an Akhanda Brahmachari.

He burnt Lanka. He gave Sri Rama's ring to Sita and brought her Chudamani to Lord Rama. He killed Akshaya Kumar, son of Ravana.

Become a Brahmachari and a hero like Hanuman. Worship Hanuman. Sing:

Jaya Jaya Sita Ram ki
Jaya Bolo Hanuman ki!

BHISHMA

Bhishma was a great hero. He was a very wise man. He was just, righteous and truthful. He did what he said, and said what he meant to do. He was a great Brahmachari.

His father was king Santanu. His mother was Ganga. He renounced the kingdom to please his father. He made a great sacrifice for the sake of filial duty.

He died at his will. He gave spiritual instructions to king Yudhishthira, lying on the bed of sharp arrows. He was a saintly warrior.

BECOME LIKE BHISHMA

Become like Bhishma, O Narendra.

My beloved Narayan! Become a Brahmachari like Bhishma or Hanuman. Be truthful like Harischandra. Be generous like Karna. Be brave like Arjuna.

Be virtuous like Yudhishthira. Be merciful like Buddha. Be devoted like Dhruva and Prahlada. Be brilliant like Brihaspati. Be a hero like Bhima. Be dutiful like Lord Rama.

Be wise like Nachiketas. Be a Yogi like Jnana Dev. Be chivalrous like Shivaji.

DRAUPADI

Draupadi was the wife of the Pandavas. She was an embodiment of duty, charity, truth, devotion, chastity and righteousness. She was the daughter of king Drupada. Dhrishtadyumna was her brother.

She in her previous life asked for the boon of a worthy husband from Lord Siva, five times. Therefore, Lord Siva declared that she would have five husbands in her next birth. She came out of the fire in a sacrifice.

Lord Krishna gave her inexhaustible cloth and protected her honour. She had intense faith in Lord Krishna. Arjuna won Draupadi in the Svayamvara.

SHINE LIKE SITA

O beloved Lila! Sita is the wife of Lord Rama. She is the daughter of king Janaka. She is the heroine of the Ramayana. She is the most virtuous and pious lady the world has ever produced. She is still a model for Indian girls. She is an Avatara of Goddess Lakshmi.

She was pure, simple and highly devoted to Lord Rama. She was an ideal wife. She was an embodiment of endurance and austerity. She was an ideal Pativrata. She faced the ordeal of fire. In Sita, beauty was blended with purity, simplicity, devotion and sacrifice.

May you all shine like Sita! May you all imbibe the virtuous qualities of Sita! May her blessings be upon you all!

LORD KRISHNA AND ARJUNA

Lord Krishna is the Lord of the three worlds. He was the Purna Avatara of Lord Vishnu. He had sixteen Kalas or rays. Arjuna was a mighty hero. He was the third son of Pandu. He was born with the Amsa or power of Indra, the Lord of Svargaloka.

Arjuna was the devoted disciple of Lord Krishna. Krishna loved Arjuna very much.

In the Mahabharata-war, Krishna drove the chariot of Arjuna. He brought success to the Pandava brothers.

Sri Krishna taught the Bhagavadgita to Arjuna in the battle-field when Arjuna was overcome with grief. He gave the Cosmic Vision or Visvarupa Darshana to Arjuna. Arjuna was the most blessed of all, because he got the Gita-Upadesa from the sacred lips of Krishna. Lord Krishna blessed the world through the medium of Arjuna. Arjuna and Krishna are Nara and Narayana.

KARNA

Karna was one of the greatest heroes of the Mahabharata. He was reputed for his extreme generosity. He was born with a natural suit of armour and with gold earrings, through the Surya-Mantra given to Kunti by Sage Durvasa. Kunti was the mother of Karna.

Kunti threw the child into the river. He was picked up by Adhiratha, the charioteer of Duryodhana. He learnt archery under Parasu Rama.

Karna was not in any way inferior to Arjuna. Sri Krishna saved Arjuna by sinking the chariot. Otherwise Karna would have killed Arjuna. Karna was killed by Arjuna in the war.

SAKUNTALA

Sakuntala was born of Menaka and Vishvamitra. Rishi Kanva was her foster-father. Sakuntala married Dushyanta. She got a promise that her son must become the heir-apparent to his throne. A son was born to them. He was known as Bharata.

Sakuntala went to the city of Dushyanta with her son and asked Dushyanta to instal Bharata as the heir-apparent. Dushyanta said, "I do not remember anything."

Dushyanta heard a voice from heaven: "Support your son. Sakuntala spoke the truth." Thereupon Dushyanta installed Bharata as his heir-apparent. Bharata became a famous king. India is called 'Bharata-Varsha', after his name.

O Madhava! Stick to your promise at any cost! Truth alone triumphs but not falsehood.

SAVITRI AND SATYAVAN

Savitri was the daughter of king Ashvapati. She was very beautiful and virtuous. She married Satyavan, the son of Dyumatsena, who was exiled from his kingdom. He was wise and heroic.

Savitri came to know from Narada that her husband would pass away within a year. She found out later her husband's death would take place on the fourth day thereafter. She observed fast for three nights.

She accompanied Satyavan to the forest. Yama came to take away his life. But Savitri fought with Yama and brought her husband back through the force of her chastity. O Sushila! Be pure like Savitri.

NALA AND DAMAYANTI

Nala was the son of Virasena, king of Nishadha, modern Berar. He was very handsome and religious. He married Damayanti daughter of Bhima, the ruler of Vidarbha, in the Svayamvara.

Nala lost all his kingdom and wealth in the play of dice. He left the kingdom wearing a single piece of cloth. Damayanti also accompanied Nala.

Nala deserted Damayanti in the forest. Damayanti stayed in the palace of Chedi. Nala became the manager of the stable of the king of Ayodhya. Damayanti was taken back by her father. There was another Svayamvara. Nala came. Nala and Damayanti were again united. Nala recovered his lost kingdom.

STORY OF DHRUVA

Once there lived a king called Uttanapada. He had two wives, Suniti and Suruchi. Suniti had a virtuous son called Dhruva. Suruchi hated Dhruva and sent him out of the royal palace. The boy was very sorry. He wanted to seek the help of God for getting another kingdom like that of his father.

Rishi Narada taught him a Mantra, "Om Namo Bhagavate Vasudevaya". Then Lord Vasudeva appeared before him. He gave the boy Divine Knowledge by mere touch.

Dhruva attained Nakshatra-Padavi through the grace of the Lord. He was eternally happy. Repeat this Mantra of the Lord daily.

STORY OF PRAHLADA

There was one Rakshasa called Hiranyakashipu. He did Tapas and got boons from Brahma. He could not be killed by any god, man or demon in the whole world. He was hating the name of God. He molested God's devotees and killed them also.

He had a son called Prahlada. Prahlada was very devoted to Lord Hari. His father beat his son and asked him not to repeat God's names. Prahlada did not care for his father. He was always thinking of God. He always sang the glories of God. His father tried to kill him, many times. But God helped Prahlada in all dangers. Hiranyakashipu went to extremes in his hatred towards Lord Vishnu. Then the Lord came in the form of a man-lion and killed Hiranyakashipu. Prahlada was saved. Become like Prahlada.

SIBI

Sibi was a Solar king. His capital city was Kasi, now called Banaras. He was famous for his generosity. He promised protection to a dove which had flown to him for shelter against a hawk.

Sibi offered his own flesh and body to the hawk in order to save the dove. When his limbs were cut off, both the hawk and the dove showed their own true forms and conferred on him many boons. He went on a golden car to the heaven.

There is no virtue greater than Karuna (compassion). The king of Kasi won heaven and deathless fame. Give protection to the weak, O my dear Siva Ram!

SABARI

Sabari was a woman of the forest-tribe of Bhils. She was devoted to Lord Rama. She was a pious woman. When Lord Rama was moving in the forest he visited

Sabari's Ashram. Sabari offered Arghya to Lord Rama and presented some fruits which she herself tasted first to see if they were sweet.

Rama accepted them with intense delight as they were given by Sabari with great devotion.

What is wanted is a loving heart. God does not want precious gifts. God becomes a slave of a true devotee who has done true self-surrender to Him.

STORY OF AMBARISHA

There was a king of the Solar line. His name was Ambarisha. He was a great devotee of Lord Vishnu. He observed Ekadasi Vrata. One day he worshipped the Lord on Dvadasi and gave a good feast to Brahmins. He also was about to take food.

Just then sage Durvasa came. The king welcomed him. The sage went for a bath in the river. He did not come for long. The king took water to keep up his Vrata as he could not take food before the sage's arrival.

Durvasa came after bath. He was very angry because the king had drunk water. He created a demon to kill Ambarisha. The Lord sent his disc, Sudarsana, to protect Ambarisha. It killed the demon. Then it went to kill Durvasa. The sage ran in fear. He took refuge in Vishnu. The Lord said He could not help him and directed him back to Ambarisha. Then Ambarisha prayed to the Lord and pacified the disc. The sage was saved by Ambarisha.

My dear children! Do not be proud of your powers or wealth. Pride leadeth to fall and disgrace.

HARISCHANDRA

Harischandra was the king of Banaras. He always spoke the truth. His name is another word for truth. He ruled the kingdom justly and wisely. His queen was Chandramati.

Rishi Visvamitra tested him in a variety of ways. Harischandra was sent out of his kingdom. He was separated from his queen. His son died of snake-bite. He was to cremate his own son. He was tempted by Visvamitra to speak falsehood. He was very adamant. He never told a lie.

Lord Siva was pleased with his truthfulness. His son came back to life. Lord Siva said, "Harischandra! You are my true Bhakta. I am pleased with you. You have never uttered even one lie in your whole life. Take back all your kingdom, wealth and property. Go back to your palace with your queen and son. Live happily. Your name will become very popular in the world. People will adore you as Truth-incarnate. May you become happy."

Aim high. Become like Harischandra. Even at the point of death do not utter falsehood. Have simple living and high thinking. May you attain glory and success!

KING VIKRAMADITYA

King Vikramaditya was the greatest of Indian kings, next only to Sri Ramachandra. He was equal to the sun in valour. His rule was humane and benevolent. His reign was called the golden age of India. He had nine gems in his court. Kalidasa was one of them. He revived the life of Sanskrit-literature. He subdued the whole of India.

There were peace, plenty and prosperity during his

rule. People did not lock their houses, and thieves were unknown. All the people were very happy. The king was a great devotee and follower of Dharma. He was a master of 64 Kalas. He had Ashta-Siddhis and Navanidhis under his power.

His throne was borne by 32 lions. He was very just, righteous and kind. Fahiang, a Chinese traveller, wrote about the rule of this king. During his reign, the country was blooming with education and culture. He attained the zenith of royal glory.

Chapter Four

EPICS AND PURANAS

THE GREAT MAHABHARATA WAR

Dhritarashtra was the father of Duryodhana. He was blind. Pandu was the younger brother of Dhritarashtra. Duryodhana was not just and virtuous. He took away the property of the Pandavas, the sons of Pandu, through gambling.

The great Mahabharata War began between the brothers. Arjuna and Bhima fought very bravely. They killed the Kauravas, the sons of Dhritarashtra.

Bhishma, the General of the Kaurava-army, was wounded by Arjuna. The Pandavas got the victory.

THE PANDAVAS

Long, long ago, there were two great kings of India called Pandu and Dhritarashtra. Pandu had five sons.

The eldest was Yudhishthira. He was just and virtuous. The second was Bhima, a very strong man. He was a great fighter. The third was Arjuna. He was an expert in archery.

Nakula and Sahadeva, the two youngest brothers, were twins. The brothers were all good, brilliant, just and virtuous. They were called the Pandavas.

THE KAURAVAS

Dhritarashtra was born blind. He had a hundred sons. Duryodhana was the eldest son.

Duhsasana was the brother of Duryodhana. He was the man who dragged Draupadi by the hair. Bhima took a vow that he would drink the blood of Duhsasana. He fulfilled his vow.

The sons of Dhritarashtra were very unjust and wicked. They were jealous of the Pandavas. They were called the Kauravas. The story of the Pandavas and the Kauravas is told in the Mahabharata.

STUDY RAMAYANA

My dear Krishna! Study Ramayana daily. You will become a good boy. Lord Rama will bless you. Lord Rama was the son of king Dasharatha. He ruled Ayodhya. His wife was Sita. Lakshmana, Bharata and Shatrughna were his brothers. Kausalya was Lord Rama's mother.

Love your brother like Lakshmana. Be brave and pure like Hanuman, servant of Lord Rama.

Visit Ayodhya. Ayodhya is a sacred place. Take bath in Sarayu river. Ask your parents to take you to Ayodhya.

ESSENCE OF RAMAYANA

Lord Rama is the Avatara of Lord Hari. He took his birth to destroy the wicked Ravana who was troubling the Rishis. Ravana was the king of Lanka, the modern Ceylon.

Lord Rama was banished by Kaikeyi, mother of Bharata. He went to Dandaka forest with his wife Sita and brother Lakshmana. Ravana came in the guise of a mendicant and took away Sita. Rama made friendship with Sugriva. Hanuman became his servant and messenger.

There was a severe battle. Rama killed Ravana and took back Sita. Rama returned to Ayodhya with his party. He was crowned as king of Ayodhya. His rule was called 'Rama Rajya'. There were peace and plenty, everywhere.

THE GITA

I

Arjuna was to fight with the Kauravas. He had Lord Krishna as his war-charioteer. Arjuna saw all his relatives facing him in war. He said to Krishna, "O Krishna! All these opponents are my dear kinsmen. I cannot commit sin. I do not want to fight with them. I cannot kill them. O Krishna! I am ignorant. I am your disciple. Teach me knowledge."

Lord Krishna said, "O Arjuna! You must fight. There is no sin. It is your Dharma as a Kshatriya. Do not neglect your duty. It is a mistake. You must follow your own Dharma till death. Think that gain and loss, happiness and sorrow, are equal.

"You must work alone. Do not think what you will get from that work. See, I am here. I am God. I am by your side. Wake up. Be cheerful. Worship Me. I am the Lord of all the worlds."

II

Sri Krishna said to Arjuna. "O hero! Offer everything that you do, to Me alone. Because I am God Myself. Do not have any mental fever. You must do the work that ought to be done. You should not have any desire for its fruits. It is real law. Then you will become a real Yogi. To leave off worship of God through flowers and water or fire, is not good. He who does not do anything is not a real Yogi. Do your prescribed duty, but do not look for its result.

"All these warriors are already killed by Me through My Divine Power. I can destroy the whole world Myself. I do not require you. You are only an instrument.

"Fix your mind on Me. Renounce egoism. God is in your heart and in all others' hearts. Take refuge in Him. I am that God. Leave all Dharmas. Come unto Me. I will give you liberation and help."

SRI KRISHNA AND UDDHAVA

Lord Krishna was about to depart from this world. His devoted minister and disciple Uddhava prayed to Him and wept before Him. He could not bear the Lord's separation. He said to the Lord, "O Krishna! Do not leave me here. I cannot live without You."

Lord Krishna said to Uddhava, "My dear friend! Do not grieve. You cannot come to Me in this state. Get yourself purified. Meditate on My Supreme Form. I am God. I am everything. I am the creator, preserver and destroyer of this world. Fleshly senses cannot perceive Me. I am beyond the perception of the mind and the intellect also.

"Go to Badrinath, My Ashram, and meditate on Me. I will take you unto My bosom."

Worship the Lord like Uddhava.

Chapter Five

HEALTH AND BRAHMACHARYA

HEALTH IS ABOVE WEALTH

Take care of your health. Do not eat much sweetmeats. Do not overload the stomach. Do not take onions, garlic, meat or fish. Take milk, fruits, Parwal, Lauki and Palak.

Take cold bath daily. Rub the body with a coarse towel. Do not daily use soap. Take a plunge-bath in the river. Run in the open air. Do Asanas regularly. Do Sirshasana, Sarvangasana, Matsyasana, Bhujangasana. Do Dand, Bhaitak. Bask in the sun, morning and evening. Do deep breathing a little.

Drink pure, filtered water. Learn hygiene a bit. Do not allow flies to sit on your food.

BRAHMACHARYA

Brahmacharya is purity in thought, word and deed. Practice of Brahmacharya will give you good health, inner strength, peace of mind, a long life and God-realisation. A perfect Brahmachari can move the whole world.

It is through the force of Brahmacharya that Lakshmana was able to kill the mighty Meghanada, son of Ravana. The great Bhishma, the grandfather of the Pandavas and the Kauravas conquered death through

Brahmacharya. Hanuman became a Mahavira through Brahmacharya.

You will have a wonderful health, through Brahmacharya. By the practice of Brahmacharya, longevity, glory, strength, vigour, memory, knowledge, wealth, undecaying fame, virtues and devotion to Truth increase. Do Japa, Kirtan, prayer, meditation, Sarvangasana, regularly. Take pure vegetarian food. You will become a powerful Brahmachari.

FAST FOR HEALTH

O Sankar! If you get pain in the stomach, do not take any food. Fast. Take a dose of castor oil. Drink a tumblerful of water. Fasting will do you immense good.

Do not stuff yourself with medicine always. Lead a natural life. Take sun-bath in the early morning and evening. Take regular exercises. Take fruits and tomato-juice. You will possess wonderful health.

Become your own doctor. Do not go to doctors. Pure air, pure water, sunlight, wholesome food are the best medicines. Be natural always.

HUMAN BODY

The human body is made up of bones, flesh, fat and blood. Various organs are placed within the cavities of the chest and belly. It receives the food and digests it. Bladder contains urine. Liver produces bile. Mind is in the brain. It thinks and feels.

The immortal soul dwells in the heart. The two eyes are the windows through which the soul sees. The body dies but the soul ever remains. You are really the immortal soul.

ALWAYS BE NEAT AND CLEAN

Cleanliness is next to godliness. Cleanliness makes you smart and active. If you are clean you will be healthy. Take a bath in cold water daily. Clean your teeth well. Put on a clean dress. Wash your cloths daily. Be clean in thought, word and action also.

Keep your room very clean. Remove all rubbish, dust and waste-paper. Sweep it daily. Many diseases will disappear.

If you are clean, your teachers will like you. All will like you. You will have a charming personality. Everybody hates a dirty man.

Keep your notebook clean. If you write your answers neatly, the examiners will be pleased with you. They will give you credit marks also.

BEST SIX DOCTORS

The best six doctors are sunshine, water, air, diet, exercise and rest. No one can deny this. These doctors do not charge you even a pie. Their treatment is ever free. Get their free treatment and be ever happy and healthy.

Sun-bath is a great tonic. It invigorates you. It gives you vitamin D and removes all skin-diseases. Sunlight is a cheap and powerful disinfectant. It kills all germs. Expose your clothing in the sun daily. Pure air will purify your blood.

Pure water gives you good health. Wholesome, light, nutritious diet will make you healthy and strong. Never take stale things, overripe and unripe fruits. Be regular in your exercise. Take rest.

ANTIDOTES FOR INDIGESTION

If you suffer from indigestion caused by eating mangoes drink milk. If you have indigestion by taking excess of ghee take lemon-juice. If you have indigestion from taking plantains, take Sambhar salt.

If you suffer from indigestion from eating cakes take hot water. If you get indigestion by taking milk take butter-milk. If you get indigestion from eating jack-fruits, take plantains.

If you suffer from indigestion from eating coconuts take a small quantity of rice. If you have indigestion from Kalai-dal take a little quantity of sugar. If you get indigestion by drinking water take a little honey. If you suffer from indigestion by taking apricots take water freely.

SUNLIGHT IMPROVES EYESIGHT

Sun is the presiding god for the eyes. He bestows health, vigour and vitality. Sit in the sun in the early morning and evening with your eyes closed. Slowly move your head from side to side. Allow the sun to shine directly on your closed eyelids, for ten minutes.

Now come in the shade. Cover the eyes with palms and the hands for five minutes. Avoid any pressure on the eye-balls.

Your eyesight will improve. There will be no necessity for wearing glasses. Practise this for one or two weeks. You can continue this for a month also.

LEARN FIRST-AID

Become a scout. Learn first-aid. You can serve people when they are in distress. Learn bandaging. Stop bleeding by means of pressure with pad of cloth or cotton and put on a bandage. If there is a cut wash it with pure water. Then use iodine or tincture benzoin (Friar's Balsam).

Use coats for a stretcher. Put ice on the bridge of the nose and back of neck if there is nose-bleeding. If there is shock, keep the body warm by covering the patient with a blanket. Give him hot coffee or tea.

Use alum solution to stop bleeding. Prepare this solution, dip a piece of cotton or clean cloth in the solution, and apply it to the bleeding part, and put on bandage.

CHEAP LIITLE DOCTORS

It is no good to run to a doctor for every minor complaint. Become a doctor yourself. Fast for a day. It will cure many diseases.

Take Triphala-powder with warm milk or water for constipation. Take honey with milk. If there is indigestion take a few small pieces of fresh ginger mixed with a little sugar as the first thing in the morning. If there is discharge of pus from the ears put garlic oil or neem oil.

If there is inflammation in the gums rub them with a little salt mixed with mustard oil. You can use this oil for rubbing in rheumatism. Expose the oil to sun. If there is cavity in the tooth apply a little camphor.

TREATMENT FOR SHOCK

Pray for the patient's rapid recovery. Do Kirtan near him. Place him flat on his back on a bed. Loosen the clothing at the neck, chest and waist to make the breathing free.

Cover the patient with warm blanket. Keep hot-water bottles to the sides and feet. Cover the bottles with a cloth. Let them not affect the skin.

Give hot coffee or tea if the patient is able to swallow. Rub gently turpentine liniment to his feet, hands and chest. Do not allow him to get up, to prevent heart-failure.

Chapter Six

MORAL LESSONS

TIME IS MOST PRECIOUS

Time is money. Time is more precious than money. Money can be earned again if it is lost. But if time is lost it cannot be regained. A moment once gone cannot be called back.

Life is but a collection of small moments. Every moment should be well utilised in study of Gita, Kirtan, Japa, Prayer, meditation, service of the poor and Mahatmas, study of class-lessons and honest earning of money. The 'tick tick' of the clock reminds you that moments are passing away.

Do not waste your time in playing chess and cards, seeing cinemas and reading novels. Realise the value of time. You will repent in old age if you misuse it. Do not kill time in idle gossiping and chit-chatting. You will become a great man if you use your time in a useful manner. Have your daily routine and stick to it. You will be crowned with success.

BE PUNCTUAL

Time is more precious. You will miss your lesson if you go to your school every day late by an hour. You will miss the train if you do not go to the station at the right time.

Form the habit of doing things at the right time. Get up early and start your work at the right hour. If you have to go to the school at 10 a.m., try to reach there always a few minutes earlier. Be punctual in attending any meeting.

See, nature is also punctual. The sun rises at the right hour. Seasons come in the right time. If you are not punctual your life will be a failure. If you are punctual it will be a great success. If you form the habit of being punctual it will always help you to do all your work at the right time.

DO YOUR DUTY WELL

Everyone has got some duty to do. Obey your parents. Your loving mother feeds you and makes you comfortable in every way. Love her. Respect her. Do willingly whatever she says, and please her. Obey your father also. Respect your noble father. He earns money for you. Father and mother take care of you. They are visible gods for you.

Learn your lessons well. Obey and respect your teachers. This is also your duty. After finishing your studies serve your mother-country. Relieve the sufferings of the poor. This is also your duty.

Respect elders. Serve neighbours. Do Sandhya-Van-dana and prayer three times a day. Your entire success in life depends upon discharging your duties well in different walks of life.

BECOME A HERO

Do not be timid. Be bold. Be cheerful. Be courageous. Walk like a lion. Talk boldly. Remove shyness. Be ever active. Take care of your health. Be strong, healthy and fiery.

Whenever you make up your mind to do certain work do it with all your heart and soul. Finish it anyhow. Do not leave it half-done. When you take a book for study, finish it.

Service and sacrifice must be your motto. Remember those great persons who have sacrificed their lives for the sake of the mother-country. Do heroic deeds which may be remembered long. Lead an exemplary life.

PROVERBS

Where ignorance is bliss, it is folly to be wise. Rome was not built in a day. Many a drop makes a mighty ocean. Take care of the pence, pounds will take care of themselves.

Slow and steady wins the race. Look before you leap. Haste makes waste. Virtue is its own reward. All work and no play makes Jack a dull boy. Be a jack of all and master of one. What you do, do it well. Man proposes, God disposes.

Kind words are better than coronets. Do unto others as you would be done by. A soft answer turneth away wrath. Take time by the forelock. Make hay while the sun shines. Unity is strength. Honest labour is honourable.

Fortune favours the brave. Failures are stepping-stones to success.

GOLDEN RULES

Obey your parents. Speak the truth always. Be punctual. Never tell a lie. Always be neat and tidy. Be good and do good. Be a hero. Help the poor and the needy. Do your daily duty well.

Learn your lessons well. Respect elders and your teacher. Serve your country. Serve society. Never shirk work. Do not put off anything for tomorrow. If you do your duty well the battle of life will be won. You will be ever happy.

Be ever active. Selfless service, sacrifice, love must be your motto. Lead an exemplary life. Be polite and courteous. Never injure the feelings of others. Never speak harsh words. Speak sweetly. Give up talkativeness. Do not abuse anybody. Do some good service everyday.

INCREASE YOUR EARNING CAPACITY

Utilise every second profitably. Be diligent and vigilant. Have an all-round development. Learn cooking. Learn typing and shorthand. Learn honest business. Learn gardening, agriculture. If there is a small garden in your backyard, grow vegetables, fruit-bearing trees.

Be very busy. Develop the power of observation. Keep company with good people. Do not waste even a single paisa. Marry only when you are able to earn your own livelihood. Lead a well-regulated, disciplined life. Crush idleness, slothfulness, back-biting, tale-bearing. Do not join parties.

In leisure hours give tuition to boys. Have a small, paying business without much capital. Have good commission agency. Save every pic. Learn art, handicraft, harmonium, violin, music.

RISE EARLY

My beloved Radha! Get up early in the morning. My dear Ram! As soon as you get up from your bed sing: "Hare Rama Hare Rama Rama Rama Hare Hare; Hare Krishna Hare Krishna Krishna Krishna Hare Hare." Do full prostration to father, mother and all elderly persons.

When you meet your friends or master in the school, say Jaya Ramji ki or Jaya Krishnaji ki, or Om Namo Narayanaya, or Jaya Sita Ram, or Jaya Radhe Shyam.

Pray before you start reading your books.

DO'S AND DON'TS

Don't play cards. Playing cards will make you a wicked boy. Do not go to cinema. But do go to the temple daily and worship the Lord. Take flowers, camphor and fruits when you go to the temple.

Don't hate anybody but do love all. Give a pie to a blind man. Wash the clothes of your parents. Never become angry towards your parents and others. Anger is very bad. It will spoil your health. You will spoil your name. You will do wrong actions if you become angry.

God watches your thoughts. Don't hide your thoughts. Be frank. Be pure in your thoughts, words and actions.

BECOME A GOOD BOY

Dear Govinda! Do not fight with your brothers and class-fellows. Obey your parents and teachers. Do not smoke. This is a bad habit. You will get disease from smoking. Give up bad company.

Do not use vulgar words. Do not abuse anybody. Be kind to all. Serve all. Love all. Respect elders. Do not steal anything. Do not hurt anybody. Speak gently. Speak sweetly. Be punctual in your school.

Study your daily lessons well. Stand first in the class. Do not play much. Do not kill bugs and scorpions. Do not waste time.

SIMPLE LIVING AND HIGH THINKING

O Mahadev! Avoid luxury. Be simple in your food and clothing. Do not multiply your wants and desires. Desire and luxury are enemies of peace and happiness. Simple living will make you happy and peaceful.

All Rishis and sages have led a simple life. They practised high thinking. They always lived in God. They were ever blissful. They had divine knowledge. They were honoured by kings.

Live in God. Do Japa. Pray. Sing Kirtan. Have sublime thoughts. Be in the company of sages and Sadhus during your holidays.

ADAPT YOURSELF

Develop adaptability. Accommodate yourself with everybody. Then only can you win the hearts of all. You will attain success in your life. If you want to adapt yourself with all, you must be humble and loving.

Arrogance, conceit and rudeness stand in the way of developing adaptability. Be gentle and soft. Be humble and simple. Obey elders. Give up obstinacy. You will soon develop adaptability.

If you possess adaptability all will love you. Your master and superior will be kind towards you. You can pull on nicely with your office-work. You will get increase of salary. You will soon become the head of a department.

BE HONEST

Even in small affairs be honest. Honesty is the best policy. Honesty is a fundamental virtue. An honest man is trusted by all. He is respected by all. He attains success in life. He soon gets promotion. He can have quick expansion in his business. He will become famous.

God will bless an honest man. Officers like an honest man. You will have a clear conscience if you are honest. If you are honest you will have good sleep and good health. The gates of heaven will be opened for you hereafter.

Do not take bribes. It is a dishonest practice. It is a great sin. You will have to suffer for the wicked action. Live within your means. Cut the coat according to the cloth. Make both ends meet. Lead a simple life. Then you do not want much money. Then you need not borrow money. Then nothing will tempt you to take bribes.

STICK TO MOTTOES

Early to bed, early to rise, makes a man healthy, wealthy and wise. Be slow to promise but quick to perform. A stitch in time saves nine. Don't cry over spilt milk. Unity is strength.

A laughter a day keeps the doctor away. Don't count the teeth of a gift-horse. Things are not as they seem to be. Pride goeth on horse-back but cometh on foot. It is easier to preach than to practise.

Prevention is better than cure. Whatever that exists is God only. All that glitters is not gold. No pains, no gains. Trust in God and do the right. Time is most precious.

BECOME A PROFESSOR

Do not become a lawyer or a police-officer. You will have to tell many lies daily. You will do many wrong actions daily. You will kill your soul. You will kill your conscience.

Become a doctor or a professor or an agriculturist. You will have many holidays if you become a professor. You can lead a peaceful religious life. You will have ample leisure daily to do Japa, Kirtan, meditation.

Take care of your lands. This will bring much money. This is independence. Doctor's profession is a noble one. But do not charge heavy bills. Give free treatment to the poor.

COLLEGE GIRL

A college-girl becomes fashionable and Europeanised. She will not cook your food. She wants a cook and a maid-servant to wash her clothes. You cannot fulfil her wants. You cannot pull on well with her.

She cannot manage the house. She will claim equality with you. She cannot look after your comforts. She wants costly sarees and various kinds of jewels. If you call her to do some work for you she will be reading novels. She will worry you to take her to cinema daily.

Marry a simple, pious girl who has a little English and vernacular education, who is born of noble and pious family, who can do all domestic duties. Marry only when you are able to earn your livelihood.

GOOD MANNERS

Good manners are the signs of good breeding. They show that you are polite and courteous. If you have good manners all will love and respect you. You will win popularity.

Learn good manners. Do not be rude, discourteous and impolite. If anyone comes to your house, say, "Jaya Ramji ki! Kindly take your seat. How could I serve you? Shall I bring some water for you to drink?"

If anyone gives you a present, say, "I thank you very much!" If you speak like this, you will create a good impression in others.

BECOME A PATRIOT

Love your mother-country just as you love your mother. This is patriotism. Mother-land is very sweet and charming. There is an indescribable grandeur about your native land.

You may live amidst luxuries and pleasures in foreign lands. You may find all sorts of comforts in life. And yet you will not be happy at heart. You will think of your sweet home and native land. You will surely remember how you passed your days in the company of your loving friends, parents, brothers and sisters.

Serve your country. Let self-sacrifice, service and love be your motto. A true patriot is ever ready to lose all and give up all for the sake of his mother-country. Glory to mother-land! Glory to India, Bharatavarsha, the land of sages and Rishis, the holy country on earth.

DIVINE INSURANCE

Insure your life with God. You will have perfect safety and security. All other Insurance companies will fail but this divine insurance company will never fail.

You need not pay any premium to the Divine Insurance Company. You will have to love God only. You will have to give your heart only to the Lord. You will get inexhaustible Divine Wealth.

Sing God's glory. Do Kirtan. Repeat His name at all times. Give up all worldly attachments. You will enjoy eternal bliss.

OBEY YOUR ELDERS

Obey your parents implicitly. Do not abuse or insult them. Do not use harsh words to them. Address them with respect. If you insult your parents you will undergo great sufferings in life.

Obey your teachers. Adore them like God. They bestow learning which is the highest gift. They remove darkness and show the real light of wisdom. Those who insult their teachers will suffer the pangs of hell.

If you obey your parents, teachers, brothers and sisters you will shine as a great man. You will get plenty of wealth, prosperity and happiness.

BE CLEAN

As socn as you get up from the bed wash your face and teeth well. Then take a bath. Pray to God. Sing Hari's name. Worship Goddess Sarasvati. She will bestow learning, wisdom and increase your power of speech. Then do other works.

Never take food before you clean your teeth and face. Keep the clothes clean. Wash your hands well before taking meals. Do not bite the nails. This is a bad habit. Keep the hands clean. Do not drench your hand with ink while writing.

Do not take meals at night on Ekadasi. Do not eat too much sweets. Do not wear gold and silver ornaments. Do not sleep on cushions. Do not waste money in purchasing fashionable things. Be very economical and simple.

CHARACTER

Possess an exemplary, moral character. There can be no real, lasting success without good character. Character is power. Without it life is a failure.

Don't cram a subject. When you study, understand the sense. Study intelligently. Then it is easy to remember what you have studied. Be very attentive when you study. Be very hopeful always. Read everything thoroughly.

Study your old lessons again and again. If you do not do so you will forget them. Try to reproduce what you have learnt in paper. Pray to the Lord daily and ask His blessings.

STUDENT-LIFE

Student-life is the best period of life. There is no family-responsibility. A student is free from family-worries. Your father and mother take care of you. The school is the place for building good character and forming good habits.

Mother also is your best teacher. She can mould your character. What the teacher teaches in one month can be taught easily by the mother at home in much lesser time.

Have a programme of your daily work. Have a time-table. Stick to it at any cost. Morning time (5 to 7 a.m.) is the best time for preparing your lessons. Do not burn the midnight oil during the examination. This will affect your health.

Play games daily. This will keep your body quite fit and vigorous.

REAL GREATNESS

Live honestly, work conscientiously. Act nobly. Try to possess a large heart. A really great man is one who possesses a large heart, great wisdom and good character.

Worldly position is nothing in the eyes of God. A poor man may become a great man, if he so desires and if he tries to attain that greatness.

Napoleon, Nelson, Lord Clive, Ramsay Mac Donald, Justice Muthu Swami Iyer, Cardinal Wolsey were born poor. They became great, through their exertion. Their glorious deeds are imperishable and their names immortal.

KEEP GOOD COMPANY

Give up the company of bad boys. Do not crack jokes with girls. Bad boys will spoil your character if you mix with them.

Do not play cards. Do not gamble. This will lead you to destruction. If you play cards you will try to steal money from your father's purse. You will acquire evil qualities one by one.

Do not eat bazar-sweets. Your health will be spoiled. You will get disease. Bazar-sweets are contaminated by flies and poisonous insects.

Do not cheat others even in play. Be fair in all games. Do not be childish. But have childlike simplicity.

DO NOT IMITATE

Do not imitate your brother if he is smoking. Do not use tobacco. Do not go to a Beedi shop. Do not purchase cigarettes for your brother. Do not chew betel-leaves.

Do not visit the cinema. You will spoil your eyes. You will become a bad boy. Your character will be spoiled by going to cinema.

Wear simple dress. Keep a tuft of hair (*choti*). Do not be shy to keep Choti. Give up fashionable dressing of hair, wearing of pants, boots, etc. These are absolutely useless, expensive and most unhygienic. Wear simple dress. Eat simple food. Avoid chillies, tamarind, tea, coffee, garlic, onion, meat, fish and other irritating food-stuffs.

Chapter Seven

SPIRITUAL INSTRUCTIONS

SPIRITUAL GUIDE

Get up at 4 a.m. from bed. Sleep for six hours at night. Do 10 Malas of Japa daily. Do Kirtan for one hour. Do twenty Pranayamas. Do Sirsha, Sarvanga, Hala and Matsya Asanas. Sit on Padmasana for Japa and meditation. Read Gita a little every day.

Spend your time in the company of the wise. Observe Mouna once a week. Do selfless service a little every day. Give much in charity. Write Mantras in a notebook. Practise physical exercise in the evening. Do not tell lies. Do not be angry. Do not keep useless company. Keep up strict Brahmacharya. Study religious books daily. Control evil habits like anger, jealousy, desire, pride.

Remember the Lord always. Fast on Ekadasi days. Eradicate bad qualities like novel-reading, visiting dramas and cinemas, coffee and tea-hotels. Develop right conduct (Yama and Niyama). Eat little. Talk little. Study more. Go to bed at 10 p.m.

Right conduct is the source of all blessedness. It is also known as Yama and Niyama. If you follow these moral rules and spiritual vows you will become a great and powerful person.

Do not injure any being—any man or animal. Speak the truth always. Do not steal the property of others. Observe celibacy. Do not accept gifts from others. This is Yama.

Be pure in body and mind. Be always happy and contented. Fast on Ekadasi days at least. Read scriptures like the Gita and do Japa. Pray to the Lord every day. This is Niyama.

There is no greater wealth than Yama and Niyama. There is no greater glory than practising Yama and Niyama. God will come to you and help you if you follow these rules.

KIRTANS

Sing these Kirtans daily in the morning:

Govinda Jaya Jaya Gopala Jaya Jaya,
Radha Ramana Hari Govinda Jaya Jaya.
Sri Krishna Govinda Hare Murare,
He Natha Narayana Vasudeva.
Narayana Achyuta, Govinda Madhava Kesava,
Sadasiva Nilakantha Sambho Sankara Sadasiva.
Radhe Govinda Bhajo Radhe Gopal,
Radhe Govinda Bhajo Radhe Gopal.
Hare Krishna Hare Ram, Radhe Govinda,
Jaya Siya Ram, Jaya Jaya Siya Ram,
Jaya Radhe Shyam, Jaya, Jaya Radhe Shyam,
Jaya Hanuman, Jaya, Jaya Hanuman.
Rama Rama Rama Rama Rama Rama Ram,
Rama Rama Rama Rama Rama Rama Ram!

Jaya Nandalala, Dinadayala,
Jaya Krishna, Jaya Hare Hare.

HAVE FAITH IN GOD

Have perfect faith in God. Have faith in the holy scriptures and the words of the great men. Have faith in your own self. Have faith in the grace of the Lord and in the power of His name.

Faith can move mountains. Faith can work wonders. Strengthen the faith if it is flickering, by contact with sages and devotees and study of holy books. Open your heart to God. Become as simple as a child.

Nama Deva had intense faith in Lord Krishna. The Lord ate the food given by Nama Deva. Prahlada had unswerving faith in the Lord Hari. The Lord saved him when he was troubled by his cruel father. Lord Siva gave Darshan to Kannappa.

POWER OF PRAYER

Prayer is a great spiritual force. Prayer should be done with faith, with a heart wet with sincere devotion. Do not argue about the efficacy of prayer. Prayer has tremendous influence.

Open freely the chambers of your heart when you pray. Have no cunningness or crookedness. You will get everything. Be regular in your prayer. Ask for light, purity, devotion and knowledge.

Draupadi prayed fervently. Lord Krishna at once relieved her from distress. Gajendra prayed fervently. Lord Hari marched with His disc to protect him. Mira prayed. Lord Krishna served her as a servant. Pray fervently right now from this very second. O Beloved Radha-Krishna! Do not delay, friend! That tomorrow will never come.

DAILY DUTY

Get up early in the morning. Sing Lord's names. Repeat Stotras. Say thus:

"Krishnam Kamalapatraksham
Punyasravanakirtanam,
Vasudevam Jagadyonim
Namami Narayanam Harim."

Wash your face. Take your bath. Do Japa of the name of the Lord. Pray to Him. Worship Him. Take your breakfast. Then go to school. Pray to God that He may give you success in your studies.

At noon, before taking food, pray to God once again. Offer your food to God and then eat. He will be pleased with you and will help you.

In the evening after your games, wash your hands, legs and face and do Japa once again. Pray to God. Sing His glories. Read His stories.

STUDY BOOKS

Dear Ram! Study well the 108 names of Lord Krishna. It is called Krishna-Ashtottara-Sata-Nama. Get it by heart. Repeat it daily.

Then study the 1000 names of Lord Vishnu. This is called Vishnu-Sahasranama. Repeat it as many times as possible. This will give you wealth, success in examination, intelligence, good health and devotion to God.

After this begin study of the Gita. Read little by little every day. Study its meaning. Lord Krishna will take care of you. He is always loving you very much. He is your constant guide. He is the Great God.

Then ask your father what is Bhagavata. He will tell you it is the story of God. It is in Sanskrit language. Study Sanskrit language and read the Bhagavata.

STUDY GITA DAILY

The Gita is the most sacred book. It contains the essence of the Upanishads. It contains 700 Slokas and 18 chapters.

Lord Krishna taught the Bhagavadgita to His devoted disciple Arjuna in the battle-field at Kurukshetra.

Maharshi Vyasa wrote this book. Get by heart one Sloka daily. Study the Gita daily. You will prosper gloriously. Keep a hand-book of the Gita always in your pocket.

MOTHER GANGA

The Ganga is the most holy river in the world. Yamuna, Godavari, Sarasvati, Narmada, Sindhu, Kaveri, Tamraparni, Sarayu are other sacred rivers.

The Ganga was brought to this world from the heavens by king Bhagiratha through his Tapascharya.

Take a bath in these sacred rivers. It will purify your heart. Repeat Ganga-Lahari Stotra and do Arati to the Ganga in the evening.

WRITE MANTRA

Sri Ram, Sri Ram, Sri Ram, Sri Ram,
Sri Ram, Sri Ram, Sri Ram, Sri Ram.

Write Sri Ram in a class notebook daily for ten minutes. You will get success in the examination. You will get plenty of money. You will possess good health.

All your difficulties will go away. This is the best medicine for any disease. You will be ever cheerful and happy.

Keep the notebook in your Puja-room. Offer flowers daily.

SERVICE IS WORSHIP

Father is your visible God. Mother is your visible God. A Sadhu is your visible God.

Serve Sadhus. Serve the poor. Serve the sick. Serve the parents. Serve the teachers. Serve friends.

Service is worship of God. Service of man is service of God. Service of the poor is the service of God. Service of parents is service of God.

Service will purify your heart and give immense joy. Give water to thirsty persons. Help your class-fellows. Make them understand what you have learnt. Help the blind in crossing the street.

Help your mother in the kitchen. Bring water from the neighbouring well or tank or river. Go to the bazar and buy vegetables and fruits. Wash the clothes of your parents, sick persons and Mahatmas.

Go to the hospital and bring medicine for your neighbours. Sweep the house. Clean the vessels. Distribute bread to the poor people, cows, birds, before you take food. Learn first-aid. Remove the thorns, glass-pieces and big stones from the road. Do not leave any work half-finished.

THEIST AND ATHEIST

Pattu is an atheist. Kittu is a theist. An atheist or Nastika is one who does not believe in the existence of God. A theist or Astika is one who believes in the exist-ence of God.

Pattu asked Kittu, "O! My dear Kittu! You always speak of God. You do Kirtan and Japa. You offer Him flowers. Where is He?" Kittu replied, "O Pattu! He is everywhere. He is in your heart. He is in all creatures."

Pattu said to Kittu, "Kittu! Please show me your God." Kittu beat Pattu with a stick and said, "Pattu! Show me your pain." Pattu replied, "I cannot show my pain but I feel it." Kittu replied, "Pattu, so is God. You will have to feel Him through Japa and meditation. I cannot show Him." Pattu became a theist from that moment.

RULES OF SPEECH

Save your lips from slip. Watch every word when you speak. Never speak ill of anyone. Do not exaggerate. Be true and accurate in your speech. Control your speech very carefully. Talk a little. Talk measured words. Give up talkative nature.

Before speaking think carefully whether what you are going to speak is true, kind and helpful. If it is not, do not speak. Mind your own business. Do not interfere with the affairs of others.

If you hear a scandal about another man, do not repeat it to others. Never wish to appear clever. Learn the virtue of silence. Do not give opinion if no one has asked you to give it. If you observe the above rules you will be peaceful and happy. People will respect and admire you. You will attain success in life.

SATSANGA

Satsanga is association or keeping company with sages, Yogins, Sannyasins, Mahatmas or devotees, and hearing their spiritual instructions. Satsanga is a safe boat that carries you to the other shore of fearlessness and Immortality.

Satsanga removes the darkness of ignorance and fills your mind with Vairagya or non-attachment or dispassion for worldly enjoyments. Satsanga is the sun that dispels the cloud of ignorance. It forces you to lead the life Divine and have strong conviction in the existence of God.

Study of holy scriptures is negative Satsanga. When you go to see Mahatmas go with fruits in hand wet with Bhakti. Do not argue with them. Sit silent and hear their Upadesha and practise them.

INNER RULER

O Sohrab! Man does various kinds of actions. When the Prana or life-breath departs from his body, it remains as a corpse on the ground. It gives very bad smell. The dead body is burnt or buried or thrown into the river.

The dead body cannot talk, cannot see or hear. Who created the body? The Creator is God. He is the Indweller. He is the Inner Ruler. It is through His power only this body moves and works. It is through His power you see, hear, smell, feel, talk, think and know.

Know Him. You will become immortal. You will enjoy Supreme Peace.

BE MODERATE

Eat less, drink more. Play less, study more. Sit less, walk more. Chat less, learn more. Sleep less, play more. Take less, give more. Speak less, act more. Weep not, laugh more.

Be good. Do good. Be wise. Be cheerful. Smile. Whistle. Jump. Dance. Pray. Laugh. Serve. Love. Give. Control. Purify. Meditate. Realise.

WHAT IS WORLD

Now! Have you seen a juggler? He will open his hand before you. There will be nothing in his hand. He will at once close it. You will see a crow or a snake coming out of his hand. When he opens his hand, it will vanish. Do you believe he has got a snake really? Certainly not. It is mere illusion or Indrajala. There is no snake.

God is the juggler. In His hand you see that there is a snake called this world. It is as vain as the snake in the hand of a juggler. At once it will vanish in no time. Suddenly it will manifest also. There is no world at all.

The spider weaves its web through what? Through its own energy, the thread. Again it gulps the thread and there is no more web. So also, God protrudes this world from Him only and draws it back to Him. Therefore world is God only. All is God and God is all. Worship all, love all, because all are God!

Chapter Eight

MORAL STORIES

A GREEDY BOY

There was a greedy boy in Amritsar. There was a narrow-necked jar in his house. It was half full of raisins. He put his hand into the jar and took a handful of raisins. But he was not able to take his hand out of the jar as his hand was full of raisins.

He tried his level best to get it out but could not succeed. He began to cry. His mother heard him crying. She came to his room and said, "What is the matter, my boy?" The boy replied, "My hand is stuck in. I can't get it out."

The mother said, "My dear boy, drop some raisins from your hand. It will come out." The boy did so and his hand came out. The mother said, "My boy, never be greedy again."

Greed makes one miserable. Therefore, O Govinda! Never be greedy. Be contented.

NEVER TELL A LIE

To tell a lie is a great sin. A liar is treated with contempt. He is not trusted by anybody. People will not believe a liar even if he speaks the truth.

Once a boy was looking after cows. He cried once, Wolf! Come for my help!" The neighbouring people ran up to him. The boy laughed and said, "No wolf! I made a fun only." He did like this thrice. A wolf actually came one day. The boy cried for help. People did not go as they thought it to be a lie. The wolf killed the boy.

Thus you see, there is great harm in telling a lie. Admit your faults. Never tell a lie. You will become bold. You will have a pure and clear heart. All will admire and love you.

A CLEVER MONKEY

A monkey lived on a coconut palm, near the river. A crocodile was his friend. The monkey used to give coconuts to the crocodile. One day the crocodile gave a coconut to his wife. She ate it and said, "My dear husband! The fruit is very palatable. I want to eat the heart of your friend, because his heart must be very palatable, as he eats the sweet coconuts."

The crocodile went to the monkey and said, "Let us go for a walk in the river." When they reached the middle of the river, the crocodile said, "My wife wants to eat your heart."

The monkey replied, "I have placed my heart on the tree." When they came back to the river-bank, the monkey jumped up on the tree and said, "My friend! You were foolish to believe me. I never leave my heart on the tree." The crocodile went back very sadly.

URMILA AND UMA

Gopichand had two daughters, by name Urmila and Uma. He loved them very much. He gave Urmila in marriage to a gardener and Uma to a potter. One day

Gopichand went to Urmila's house and said, "How are you my darling?" Urmila replied, "We are very happy. Please pray that our plants may get water."

Then Gopichand went to Uma's house and said, "How are you my beloved Uma?" She replied, "We are happy. Please pray that there should not be any rain for some days so that our earthen-pots may get dry."

Now Gopichand was in a fix. He could not decide for whom he should pray. He reflected deeply and found out that everybody in the world is selfish.

WISDOM OF BUDDHA

Once the son of a poor woman died. She went to Lord Buddha and asked him to give her some medicine to bring back her child to life. Buddha told her, "O lady! There is only one medicine which could bring back your son to life. Bring me a handful of mustard from a house where there has been no death."

The poor woman went from door to door and asked for a handful of mustard. She received the same reply at every door. One said, "I have lost my son." Another said, "My father died yesterday." A third said, "My wife died last month."

She returned to Buddha with a sad heart and narrated everything. Then Lord Buddha replied, "Do not think much of your own grief. Sorrow and death are common to all."

ANT AND GRASSHOPPER

In days long gone by there lived two neighbours. One was an ant and the other a grasshopper. The ant was very active. He was hard-working too. He was always busy in storing up grains of rice for the winter.

His neighbour, the grasshopper was very idle. He passed the summer happily in singing. The winter came. He had nothing to eat. One day he went to his neighbour and begged him for food. The ant asked, "My friend, how did you spend the summer?" The grasshopper replied, "In singing!" The ant replied, "Spend the winter in dancing. Sorry, I can't spare you anything."

The poor grasshopper returned home with a sad heart. He spent the whole winter starving.

Moral:—Never sit idle. Be ever active and busy. Always save something for the future. Never beg or borrow.

AUTOBIOGRAPHY OF LADDU

I am laddu. I am very sweet and delicious. All love me very much. I am liked very much by children. Their mouth waters when they see me and hear my name. There is no big Bhandara or marriage-feast without me. Sadhus simply devour me voraciously.

I make a crying child laugh and dance in joy. I give life to a weak man. I become fat and flesh and shine in the cheeks and skin. People take great care of me. They keep me in good boxes and almirahs and big costly vessels. I increase the value of sugar, ghee and flour of gram.

The Indweller in me is Atman or God. I cannot live without Him. If people love Him in the same way as they love me, they would have attained eternal bliss long long ago.

THE RACE OF LIFE

Once there was a boy called Ramu. One day he went for bath in the river Ganga. At once an elephant came running to kill him. The boy was afraid. He ran inside the pot Gangasagar (a pot with a narrow spout and a wide mouth). The elephant followed him inside the Gangasagar. The boy came out of the spout. The elephant also came out through the spout but its tail was caught in the spout. It lost the tail.

The boy climbed up a Tulasi plant. But his tuft (hair) was hanging down. The elephant caught hold of the tuft and climbed. The boy cut off the hair and the elephant fell down dead.

O Govinda! The river is the life of passions and desires. The boy is the Jiva. The elephant is the Maya. Gangasagar is the life of renunciation. The spout is cave-life. The plant is the plant of life. The hair is the tuft of old Vasanas. Cut off the Vasanas. Maya will fall off. You will attain peace by erasing the old Samskaras.

TRUE FRIENDSHIP

Dionysius king of Syracuse in Sicily, sentenced Pythias to death. Pythias said to the king, "I will go home and settle my domestic affairs and return on the day of execution." Dionysius said, "How can I be sure of your return?"

Damon, friend of Pythias said to the king, "I will remain as a prisoner in place of Pythias. If he does not return, I can be hanged." The king allowed Pythias to go home. Damon was taken prisoner in his place. Pythias reached his native place and settled his domestic affairs.

There were severe winds also. Pythias did not come in time. Damon was led to the gallows for being executed.

Pythias came riding on a horse to the spot with great speed. The king said to the executioner, "Stop! They shall not die. They have taught me a lesson in faithful friendship. I wish I would become a third in this bond of true friendship."

THE DOG IN THE MANGER

A dog once sat in a manger which was filled with straw. An ox came to the manger to eat the straw. The ox said, "My dear dog! The straw is of no use to you. Please allow me to eat it." The dog replied, "The straw is of no use to me. I can't eat it. Why should you also eat it?"

The dog was very selfish. There are many students, children and human beings also who are very selfish like the dog. They want everything for them. They do not care for the interests of others. They do not wish that others also should be benefited. A selfish man or student believes that he only is right and all others are wrong.

Kill selfishness. Try to look from another man's point of view. Be unselfish. Try to make others happy. Share what you have with other children. Look after the interests of others. You will be happy. You will become a great man.

GIVE UP GREED

Once a woman missed the train. She was forced to stay in the second-class waiting-room at night. She had a lot of money and ornaments with her. The son of the station-master turned the woman out and slept on the sofa. She slept quietly in the inter-class waiting-room.

The station-master was a greedy person. He sent the watchman to murder the woman and take away the cash and ornaments. The watchman murdered the boy lying on the sofa. The boy cried.

The station-master came there and saw his son lying in a pool of blood. They threw the corpse on the railway line.

The train arrived. The engine-driver stopped the train. The police was sent for. An enquiry was made. The lady told the whole story. The station-master and the watchman were arrested.

Greed brings destruction.

THE WOLF AND THE LAMB

A wolf was drinking water in a river. A lamb was also drinking water down below. The wolf wanted to eat the innocent lamb. The wolf approached the lamb and said, "You rascal, why are you polluting the water that I drink?"

The lamb replied politely, "Venerable Sir! How can I spoil the water? The water is flowing from you to me." "You abused me nine months back", said the wolf. The lamb replied, "I was not born then, Sir!" Then the wolf said, "Then it must be your mother." Thereupon the wolf tore the lamb into pieces and ate it up.

It is very easy to find fault with others. There are many wolves among boys and men also. Mischievous boys and men who hurt others are really wolves. Remove the brute in you. Be good, and do good.

RAJAMANI

Rajamani was a native of Madura. He was studying in the fifth class. He had father, mother, two brothers, an old grandfather and grandmother.

The grandfather, Pichumani was aged eighty. Pichumani loved Rajamani very much. He gave him whatever he wanted. He often called Rajamani for some service. Rajamani disliked his grandfather because he called him very often for some service. He could not even find time for play. One day a friend of his came to play in the evening. Pichumani asked Rajamani to bring some hot water for his bath. Pichumani was half blind. He could not move about freely.

Rajamani got annoyed. He took the boiling kettle of water and poured it over the old man's head. His whole body was blistered.

O Govinda! Do not act like Rajamani. Be obedient. Service of parents and aged is your foremost duty. Then will you be really happy, prosperous and peaceful.

MIND YOUR OWN BUSINESS

There was a mischievous monkey. One day it went on skipping and playing in the woods. There was a log of wood which was half cut by the saw. The workers had put a round stick inside the sawn portion. The wood was giving a space near that stick.

The monkey went and sat near the stick. It wanted to pull out that stick. It was strong. It somehow tried its best and took it out. But the two sawn pieces of wood suddenly joined together and the monkey's testicles were crushed in no time. The monkey shrieked and died.

Do not meddle with the affairs of others. Mind your own business. Do not give your own opinions. Be humble in nature. Talk little, think more.

SELF-RELIANCE

A lark lived in a field of corn, with her young ones. It went out in the morning to bring some food. It said to the young ones: "Tell me whatever may happen in my absence." In the evening they told her that the owner requested his friends to reap his corn.

The mother said, "Don't worry. We are quite safe here." On another day the children said that the owner requested his neighbours to reap the corn. The mother said, "My dear children! There is no danger now." On another day the children said that the next day the owner with his son would come and reap the corn. The lark said, "Now there is danger. We must move to a safe place without delay. The owner will surely come tomorrow, because it is his own work."

If you wish to see a work well done, do it yourself. Do not depend upon others. You do the eating yourself. You do not depend upon others.

PARENT-WORSHIP

Worship of parents is equal to worship of God. Goddess Parvati, mother of Ganesha and Subrahmanya, kept a nice fruit in front of them and said, "He who goes round the world and comes first can take this fruit."

Subrahmanya sat on his peacock and drove fast to make a round around the world. Ganesha went round

Lord Siva and Parvati thrice and demanded the fruit. Parvati gave the fruit and Ganesha ate it.

Subrahmanya came after three days going round the world and found that Ganesha had eaten the fruit. It was then that Subrahmanya realised the glory of parent-worship.

A DIVINE HERB

Two schoolboys Siva and Rama were each carrying a heavy basket for their teacher. Siva murmured and complained that his basket was very heavy. Rama laughed and was happy as if his basket was light.

Siva said, "O Rama! How are you able to laugh? Your basket is as heavy as mine. You are weaker than me also." Rama replied, "I have put in my basket a small herb which decreases the weight."

Siva asked, "O Ram! Do tell me, what is this herb? I too want to put that herb in my basket to decrease the weight." Rama replied, "O Siva! My dear friend, the most valuable divine herb which makes every burden light is patience."

Chapter Nine

GENERAL KNOWLEDGE

WHO IS A SADHU?

A Sadhu is a very good man. He has no attachment for the world. He may live in a forest or in the world. He wants just enough food to keep him alive. He wears very simple dress. He has no family and children and property. And yet he is extremely happy.

He is wise and virtuous. He possesses divine qualities such as mercy, universal love, truthfulness, purity, etc. He has control over his mind and senses.

He is free from anger, greed, pride, jealousy. He loves all. He always prays and meditates. He never does any harm to anybody. People respect and adore him.

ANCIENT RISHIS

A Rishi is a great soul. A Rishi is God Himself. Vasishtha, Vyasa, Visvamitra, Valmiki are great Rishis. Vyasa is a Brahma-Rishi. Janaka is a Raja-Rishi. Kasyapa, Atri, Bharadvaja, Visvamitra, Gautama, Jamadagni and Vasishtha are the Sapta-Rishis. You can see the Sapta-Rishi-Mandala in the sky at night.

Vyasa wrote the Mahabharata and the eighteen Puranas. Valmiki wrote the Ramayana.

Make prostrations to these Rishis daily. Say *"Om*

Namah Parama Rishibhyo, Namah Parama Rishibhyah."
They will bless you.

FIVE ELEMENTS

God created the five elements—earth, water, fire, air and ether. Your physical body is also made up of five elements. Each element has a presiding God.

There are five Jnana-Indriyas or organs of perception in this body. They are ears, skin, eyes, tongue and nose. Ears hear sounds. Skin feels heat and cold. Eyes see forms and colours. Tongue tastes food. Nose smells odours.

There are five Karma-Indriyas or organs of action. They are organ of speech, hands, feet, anus and genitals. Mind is the commander of all the senses. It is the eleventh organ. Above mind is the Immortal, all-blissful Soul or Atman. He is the Inner Ruler or Antaryamin.

THE HIMALAYAS

The Himalayas are the biggest mountains in the world. Mount Everest is the highest peak in the Himalayas. Himavan is the king of the Himalayas. Parvati is the daughter of Himavan. Lord Siva married Parvati. He dwells in Mount Kailas which is in Tibet.

The Ganga, the Yamuna, the Sindhu and the Brahmaputra take their origin from the Himalayas. There are many caves in the Himalayas. Rishis and Sadhus live in the caves and do Tapas and meditation.

Visit Rishikesh and Haridwar during your summer vacations. You can see the Himalayas and the Ganga. There are very beautiful places with charming scenery.

There are many Ashrams in Rishikesh and Haridwar. Sadhus and Sannyasins live in the Ashrams.

THE VEDAS

There are four books called the Vedas. You must study these books if you wear a holy thread. Rigveda, Yajurveda, Samaveda and Atharvaveda are the four Vedas. The Vedas speak about the Truth of God. The Vedas are the embodiment of true knowledge.

The Samhitas are the Stotra-portions of the Vedas. The Brahmanas are the Yajna-portions of the Vedas. The Aranyakas are the Upasana-portions of the Vedas. The Upanishads are the Jnana-portions of the Vedas. You must study all these books.

If you have no holy thread, you read the Santi-Parva and the Anusasana Parva of the Mahabharata. Vyasa-Maharshi wrote this for you only. Study it well. You will become very intelligent.

THE WORLD

Asia, Europe, Africa, America and Australia are the five continents of this world. The Pacific Ocean, Atlantic Ocean, Indian Ocean, Arctic Ocean and Antarctic Ocean are the five Oceans of this world.

Asia contains the countries of Russia, China, Japan, India, Arabia, Persia, Afghanisthan and Mesopotamia. Europe contains many small countries. Africa has a big desert called the Sahara. In Africa there are gold and diamond mines in the south. There are many Negroes and fierce lions.

There are two lands, North and South America. The

northern land is very rich and advanced in culture. There are the famous United States.

Australia is a big island far to the south. The Arctic and the Antarctic regions are very cold. Man cannot live there.

This world is a theatre of many changing plays. There are good and bad people. There is heat and cold, hunger and thirst, day and night. There are rich and poor people. O Ram! Do not believe this world. Pray to God always who is above this world.

INDIA

This land or country is called Hindusthan or India. It is also called Bharata-Varsha. It is rich in material and spiritual wealth. The ancient people of India were advanced in real education and real culture. India's boundaries are the Himalayan Mountains in the North, the Bay of Bengal in the East, the Indian Ocean in the South and the Arabian Sea in the West. India's great rivers are the Ganges, Sindhu, Brahmaputra, Yamuna, Narmada, Godavari, Krishna and Kaveri.

Chandragupta, Ashoka, Vikramaditya, Harsha, Akbar, were some of the great Indian Rulers. They ruled in North India. The land to the south of the Vindhyas is called South India. It is called Karma Bhumi. But Uttara-Khanda is Punya Bhumi.

India has a good climate. Rice is the staple food. In the North wheat is grown. The northern people have good emotional heart. The southern Indians have good intellectual brain. Rice gives intellectual power. Wheat gives physical power.

THE FOUR YUGAS

The four Yugas are Krita, Treta, Dvapara and Kali. This is the Kali Yuga. This is the last Yuga or age. The next age will be Krita Yuga.

In the Krita Yuga people observed perfect Dharma, with truth, compassion, penance, charity. They realised God through meditation.

In the Treta Yuga Dharma loses one part called truth. They realise God through sacrifices.

In the Dvapara Yuga Dharma loses truth and compassion. They realise God through service.

In the Kali Yuga Dharma has only charity as its limb. They realise God through singing the Name of the Lord.

THE BIGGEST

The Mississippi is the longest river in the world. Mount Everest is the highest mountain. Sahara is the widest desert. Victoria is the great water-fall. Niagara is the most developed electricity- generating centre. The Pacific is the largest ocean.

The Mahabharata is the biggest Epic. The Veda is the oldest scripture. The elephant is the biggest animal. Verkhoyansk is the coldest place. Kohinoor is the biggest diamond. Asia is the largest continent.

Knowledge is the most precious wealth. Love is the best unifier. Sense-control is the greatest strength. Fasting is the best medicine. Brahmacharya is the greatest Tapas. Japa is the greatest Yajna. Rama is the greatest king. Vasishtha is the greatest Rishi. Krishna is the greatest Yogi (and Jnani). God is the greatest Being.

GREAT INVENTORS

Watt (England) is the inventor of steam-engine in 1565. Marconi (Italy) is the inventor of wireless in 1896. Madame Curie of France founded Radium in 1903. J.L. Baird (England) invented Television in 1925.

Torricelli (Italy) invented barometer in 1643. Roentgen (Germany) invented X-ray machine in 1895. Fahrenheit (France) invented thermometer in 1721. Galileo invented telescope.

Wright Brothers. (America) invented aeroplane in 1903. Edison (America) invented gramophone in 1877. Morse (America) invented electric telegraph in 1835. Bell (America) invented telephone in 1876. Daguerre and Niepge (France) invented photography.

RIDDLES

Where do you see rivers without water and towns without men? On the map. What is it that jumps to your shoulders as soon as you catch hold of its leg. Umbrella. When, I walk, I live, When I stand I die. Tell me what I am? Clock.

Which is the oldest table in the world? Multiplication table. What is that which has three feet but no legs. A yard-measure. What is that which nobody wishes to have and nobody likes to lose? A law-suit. What four letters would frighten a thief? O.I.C.U.

What is the longest word in English? Disestablishmentarianism. What is the difference between a Prince of Wales and a football. One is heir to the throne; the other is thrown to the air. What is the difference between a naughty boy and a medicine? One wounds the heel; the other heals the wound.

I.C.S. IN SUMMER

Lord Vishnu was the Governor of Bombay. Takore went to Vishnu and said, "Good morning, your Excellency! I want the job of a Collector." Lord Vishnu said, "Who are you?" Takore replied, "I am an I.C.S. in summer and P.C.S. in winter."

Lord Vishnu said, "What do you mean by I.C.S. in summer and P.C.S. in winter?" Takore replied, "I am an ice-cream-seller in summer and potato-chip-seller in winter."

The governor called his Chaprasi (peon) and said, "Chaprasi Lakshman! Turn this I.C.S. out at once. Tell him there is no job for him." Lakshman necked the I.C.S. out at once.

MAN

Man is the most excellent and noble creature in this world. He is the Marvel of marvels. He is microcosm, a little world. He is the image of God. In essence he is God.

He is the only social animal who laughs, weeps and walks and who knows what is right, what is wrong. He is the sole commander and governor of all the creatures contained in this world.

Eating, sleeping are common in animals and man. But man attains divine knowledge and becomes one with God.

THE BEST THINGS

Knowledge of Atman or the Soul is the best education. The best victory is the victory over one's mind. The best music is the music of the Soul or Anahata sounds. The best medicine is cheerfulness.

The best war is the war against your own senses and the mind. The best science is the science of soul. The best doctor is fasting. The best philosophy is not to hurt others. The best rule is to observe the golden medium.

The best mathematics is selfless service, which doubles your happiness and divides the worst sorrows. The best engineering is building a bridge of faith in God over the river of death. The best art is to sing Maha Mantra melodiously. The best study is "Enquire who am I and be free."

MAN IS SUPERIOR

Man is superior to all living beings, because he has knowledge. He knows what is right, what is wrong; what is good, what is bad.

He can cross the big ocean in ships and can fly in the air in aeroplanes. He can dive in the seas. He can talk to his friends who are living in distant places.

He can become a great Yogin or a sage. He is endowed with the powers of reasoning, enquiry, discrimination and reflection.

HINDU SCRIPTURES

Hindu scriptures are of six kinds, viz., 1. Srutis, 2. Smritis, 3. Itihasas, 4. Puranas, 5. Agamas and 6. Darshanas.

The Srutis include the four Upa-Vedas, the six

Angas, and the four Vedas containing the Samhitas, Brahmanas, Aranyakas and Upanishads.

The Smritis are many like Manu, Yajnavalkya, Parasara. The Itihasas are Ramayana, Yoga-Vasishtha, Mahabharata, Harivamsha. The Puranas are eighteen in number. The Bhagavata is the most important of all. There are many minor Puranas also.

The Agamas are manuals of worship. The Pancharatra is the most famous Agama. The Tantras are included in the Agamas.

There are six Darshanas, viz., 1. The Nyaya, 2. Vaiseshika, 3. Sankhya, 4. Yoga, 5. Mimamsa and 6. Vedanta. The Vedanta of Badarayana is the most important of all philosophies.

These embody the entire Hindu religion.

NUMBERS

One is the God that rules this universe. One is the Sun that illumines this world.

Two are the Ashwin-brothers. Two are the divisions in humanity (man and woman).

Three are the gods in Hinduism proper. Three are the Vedas that make up Brahmanism.

Four are the Varnas and four are the Ashramas. Four are the Avasthas of existence (Jagrat, etc.).

Five are the sacrificial fires. Five are the elements of nature.

Six are the seasons belonging to time. Six are the Angas (limbs) of the Veda.

Seven are the great Maharshis. Seven are the tunes in music.

Eight are the limbs of Raja Yoga. Eight are the Siddhis of perfection.

Nine are the treasures. Nine is the last number.

THE FIRST

The first of God's creations was water. The first sound produced in this universe was of OM. The first Mantra, a Brahmin is initiated into, is the Gayatri. The first king of this world was Prithu.

The first poem ever written is the Ramayana. The first man who went to America was Columbus. The first printing press was started in Germany. The first thing that pulls on life is faith.

The first thing a spiritual aspirant should avoid is evil company. The first Westerner who came to India was Vasco-De-Gama. The first Indian who became a governor was Lord Sinha.

The first man who committed sin was Adam. The first cause of misery is ignorance. The first of Hindu scriptures is the Rig-Veda. The first of all spiritual Sadhanas is Japa.

THE SUN

O Vasudev! Look at this brilliant sun. It discharges its duty in a very orderly manner. It is very punctual in rising. Be punctual like the sun. The rising sun has no rays in the beginning.

It burns or shines without oil and wick. It is endowed with inexhaustible energy and power. The Creator of sun is God. It gives you warmth in winter. It generates clouds and brings rain. All plants and trees grow on account of the sun. If there is no sun you will die of cold.

It fills your heart with joy when it rises and sets. It gives you good health, vigour and good eyesight. Study Aditya-Hridayam daily in the morning, particularly on Sundays. You will attain success in life, good health and long life. Offer Arghya to the sun morning and evening.

SEVEN WONDERS OF THE WORLD

The Taj Mahal at Agra, the leaning tower of Pisa, the hanging garden of Babylon, the pyramids of Egypt, the Colossus at Rhodes, the great wall of China and the peacock-throne of Shah Jahan are the seven wonders of the world.

The Taj Mahal was built over the tomb of Mumtaz Begum, the queen of Shah Jahan. The leaning tower of Pisa in Italy is a high tower slanting in position. It was used by Galileo for his experiments.

The garden at Babylon is floating on water. The pyramids in Cairo are huge structures of stones. The Colossus is a gigantic figure at the Constantinople harbour with its two legs on either side of the harbour.

The Wall of China was built between Mongolia and China. It is the biggest wall in the world. The Peacock-throne was famous for its workmanship and embroidery.

Mind is another great wonder. But the Wonder of wonders is your own Immortal Soul.

HINDUISM

Hinduism is the religion of the Hindus. The Rishis

and Munis of India are founders of this religion. Vedas are the sacred books of the Hindus. Hinduism says, "Be good. Do good. Do your duty to God and man. Be pure. Be simple. Worship God. Surrender to Him. Hate not anyone. All creatures are forms of God. Speak truth. Do not injure any living being in thought, word or deed."

There are four Vedas. There are 18 Puranas. Sage Vyasa composed the 18 Puranas and the Mahabharata. He also edited the Vedas. Mahabharata is known as the fifth Veda. Ramayana, Bhagavata and Bhagavadgita are the popular text-books of the Hindus.

A Hindu worships God. He worships Lord Rama, Lord Krishna, Lord Siva or Devi. He visits the temple every day. He does worship.

Chapter Ten

SIVANANDA'S LETTERS

KEEP DAILY ROUTINE

O Children of Light!

Salutations. Om Namo Bhagavate Vasudevaya.

Hope all of you are keeping good health. Now probably you are preparing for a programme as to how you will pass the summer vacation. But remember, do not while away all your time in play or useless talks. You can do one thing; make out a daily routine and stick to it throughout the vacation. Early in the morning, say at 4.30, you get up from bed and utter the Name of the Lord. Wash your hands and feet and say your prayer, sing Bhajan for at least half an hour. Then go to study. Make out a daily routine how you will study on different days. Say, after two and a half hours' study take some milk and biscuits or the like. Then assist your mother, or others in the household in their duty. Then take your bath, and then take the Lord's Name, say for fifteen minutes. Take your meals. Don't take too much, even if it is most palatable to you. This will make you drowsy and your health will not be fit. Rest for an hour. Again go to your study and do all the home-work you are to do for the day. Take a little rest, and during the rest you can talk with your parents or brothers and sisters on healthy and divine subjects. In the afternoon you must go out for play. Just before evening go out for a walk. In the evening wash your hands and feet and pray for half an hour, and then go to study. Then take your night-meals. Take rest or stroll for fifteen minutes. By 9.30 at night go to bed, but before that, you should pray to God for at least 15 minutes, and think about God while in bed.

'Early to bed and early to rise,

Is the way to be healthy, wealthy and wise.'

Read the lines of poetry ten times, and repeat it. Can you do without seeing it again? Only getting by heart will not do; you must do what you say.

Then you will be a very good child, loved by all. God will love you. May God bless you.

—Sivananda.

BE INDUSTRIOUS

O Children of the Divine Mother!

Adorations. Om Namo Narayanaya.

Hope you are well. I think you have enjoyed the summer vacation nicely. Just tell me how you have spent it? Is it all play and no study? No, I don't think you are a naughty child. Hope you have studied your lessons well, besides playing. Is it not? Also helped your parents, brothers, sisters and playmates, too? Now I shall narrate a nice story.

There were two boys who were neighbours. One was a rich man's son, Dulal, and the other was a poor, named Gopal. Both the boys read in the same class of the same school. Dulal had tutors at home but Gopal had none; so he had to work very hard to prepare his lessons.

In spite of two tutors, Dulal liked to play more than to study; so he could not become a good student.

Now during the summer vacation Gopal worked hard and completed all his lessons. But Dulal whiled away the time in play. When the school reopened after summer vacation the examination was held. When the result was out, it was found that Gopal stood first in his class and Dulal got plucked.

Don't be like Dulal, but be like Gopal. Always make your lessons complete before you go to play. Then you will become a very good child and will be loved by all.

May God bless you to become a good child.

—Sivananda.

THE PROUD CROW

Here is a story about a proud crow. On account of its pride it lost its bread. Once a proud and silly crow sat on the top of a tree. It had a piece of bread in its beak. A sly and hungry jackal saw it. He wished to have the bread-piece for himself. But the crow was on the top of the tree. So the jackal thought of a plan. The jackal said, "What a beautiful bird I find on the tree! Has he come down from heaven? But what a pity! So beautiful a bird, but he cannot sing. If he could only sing, how he could charm everybody!"

The silly crow was very proud to hear the words of the jackal. So it thought that it would sing, so that the jackal might know that it could sing, too. Then the crow cawed, and the bread-piece fell from its beak. The sly jackal ate it heartily, and said, "What a foolish and proud crow you are!"

Do not be proud when others flatter you. If you are proud, people will easily deceive you. Pride goes before a fall! Be without pride, people will like you much. God bless you!

—Sivananda.

A GREEDY DOG

O Children of Divinity!

Adorations. Om Namah Sivaya.

Today I wish to tell you a story of a greedy dog. Once there was a greedy dog. He had no food for some days. One day luckily, he got a piece of meat. With it he went by the side of a pond, to eat it with relish. But as he looked at the water he found his own shadow in it. He thought that another dog had come with a piece of meat in his mouth. As he was greedy he thought to snatch that meat also, so that he could have his belly full with two pieces. He jumped into the water to snatch away the other one. But as he jumped, his own meat fell from his mouth into the water, and was lost. Thus, he being too greedy, lost his own meat.

Do not be greedy. If you be greedy you will have to suffer. Nobody will like you. Rather share what you have with others. Then everybody will love you. God gives more to him who gives his share to others.

May God bless you. May you be happy. May you be loved by all.

—Sivananda.

DO NOT BE NARROW-MINDED

O Children of Divine Light!

Adorations. Om Namo Bhagavate Vasudevaya.

I am happy to be of any assistance to you. Respect and obey your parents, elders, teachers and saints. Study the Gita, and practise it. This is Life Divine.

Do not be narrow-minded. Now I shall tell you a story. This will show you that it is not good to be narrow-minded. A foolish devotee had a golden image of Buddha which she took wherever she went. She came to a monastery where many images of Buddha were kept. She did not like the other Buddhas; she liked only her own. Whenever she burnt incense before her image she never liked that the fumes should go to the others. She drew a curtain round the image. In a few months her Buddha, due to the fumes became dark and grim, while the others were shining still.

Similar is the case with the narrow-minded persons. They do not honour the faiths of others. But God remains in all faiths. The narrow-minded man does not know this, and so he hates others' faith. So he is not loved by God. In real faith, there are truth, purity and love. Never be narrow-minded.

—Sivananda.

Chapter Eleven

CHILDREN'S SONGS

Now, I shall give you some very good *Children's songs.* Can you get them by heart? If you can do it quickly, you are the best boy.

THE BODY

Two little eyes to look to God,
Two little ears to hear His words,
Two little feet to walk His ways,
Two little lips to sing His praise,
Two little hands to do His will,
And one little heart to love Him still.

BE A GOOD CHILD

1. Serve your parents.
2. Serve your teachers.
3. Serve the sick.
4. Serve the poor.
5. Serve with love.
6. Serve and pray.
7. Serve with eagerness.
8. Serve selflessly.
9. Serve God in all.
10. Thus serving, you will be a good child.

WORDS OF WISDOM

Health is wealth.
Time and tide wait for no man.
Waste not, want not.
Spend, and God will send.
All's well that ends well.
Count not your chickens till they are out of the shell.
A stitch in time saves nine.
It takes two to make a quarrel.
"Do it now."

YOU WILL SEE GOD

1. Think of God.
2. Speak of God.
3. Chant the Name of God.
4. Sing the song of God.
5. Love God.
6. Worship God.
7. Pray to God.
8. Weep for God.
9. Cry for God.
10. Then you will see God.

GEMS OF KNOWLEDGE

G—Give to the needy, and God will give you.
E—Expect not the fruit, it will come of itself.
M—Miserable are those who are greedy.
S—Service is worship.
O—One who saves not, earns naught.
F—Face difficulties boldly.
K—Keep a paisa by for the rainy day.
N—Nothing exists except Truth.

O—Overeating is dangerous.
W—Waste not, want not.
L—Love begets love.
E—Everything looks beautiful in its season.
D—Deeds are fruits, words are but leaves.
G—Great display, little cost.
E—Every day has its night.

DO'S AND DON'TS

Do you wish to be a most beloved child? If so, then—
Be simple.
Be gentle.
Be noble.
Be cheerful.
Be truthful.
Be graceful.
Be faithful.
Be liberal.
Be patient.
Be unselfish.
See no evil; hear no evil; speak no evil; do no evil.
Be pure in word; be pure in thought;
Be pure in feeling; be true to yourself.
'I slept and dreamt that life is beauty;
I woke and found that life is duty.'

Read the above ten times. Close the book. Can you repeat it now?

DON'T

Don't hate.
Don't worry.
Don't vex others.

Don't keep bad company.
Don't blame others.
Don't sit idle.
Don't use bad words.
Don't be angry.
Don't be greedy.
Don't tell lies.
Then you will be a very good child.

YOU WILL BE A GOOD CHILD

Eat a little.
Drink a little.
Talk a little.
Sleep a little.
Serve a little.
Give a little.
Help a little.
Worship a little.
Do Japa a little.
Do Kirtan a little.
Then you will be a good child.

I must not play
            Night and day;
I will do my duty.
            And be happy and gay.

Read the above poem ten times. Can you repeat it
without seeing it? No, only repetition will not do. Can you
do what you say? This is Divine Life.

If you want to be good:—
        See what is good.
        Hear what is good.
        Think what is good.

Act what is good.
Speak what is good.
Read what is good.
Write what is good.
Eat what is good.
Drink what is good.

GOD WILL LOVE YOU INTENSELY

Pray devotedly.
Pray unselfishly.
Pray fervently.
Pray sincerely.
Pray mentally.
Pray heartily.
Pray guilelessly.
Then God will love you intensely.

GOD IS EVERYTHING

1. God is in you.
2. God is in everybody.
3. God is in everything.
4. God is Life.
5. God is Light.
6. God is Truth.
7. God is Beauty.
8. God is Peace.
9. God is Fullness.
10. God is Love.

Chapter Twelve

MAXIMS

Children! Here are a few maxims. Try, how many you can memorise in a day. This is a good exercise for developing memory-power. If you memorise all, your memory-power is excellent. A dozen—very good. Nine—good. Six—fair. Test yourself!

SPARKS OF WISDOM

C—Charity begins at home.

H—Haste makes waste.

I— It takes two to make a quarrel.

L— Love is a great healer.

D—Do not carry coals to Newcastle.

R—Rome was not built in a day.

E—Early to bed and early to rise make you healthy, wealthy and wise.

N—No pains, no gains.

S—Self-praise is no recommendation.

C—Cut the coat according to the cloth.

O—Out of sight, out of mind.

R—Repentance is amendment.

N—No rose without a thorn.

E—Empty vessels make much noise.

R—Rolling stones gather no moss.

SIVA'S Â B C FOR CHILDREN

I

A—Always depend on God.

B—Bear insult, bear injury.

C—Control the tongue.

D—Do not cheat anybody.

E—Evil company is dangerous.

F—Fear nothing.

G—Give, give, give; God will love, love, love.

H—Helping others is a virtue.

I—Injury is a vice.

J—Japa is your coat of arms.

K—Knowledge is the fruit.

L—Live for others.

M—Mind deceives; beware!

N—Nip anger in the bud.

O—Overcome greed by liberality.

P—Pure mind is your friend.

Q—Quietness will lead you to progress.

R—Recite the Name of God.

S—Speak sweetly, speak softly.

T—To love is to serve.

U—Understand yourself.

V—Virtue is the staff of life.

W—Within you is Bliss.

X—(E)xert yourself for good.

Y—Your treasure is God.

Z—Zero has no value if not attached to a unit; so life has no value if not attached to God.

II

A—A friend in need is a friend indeed.

B—Better late than never.

C—Cheat not anybody even mentally.

D—Do as you would be done by.

E—Every lie will drag you to tell other lies.

F—Failure is a stepping-stone to success.

G—God sees your heart, not appearance.

H—He who gives, enjoys happiness.

I—It is never too late to mend.

J—Just as you sow, so shall you reap.

K—Keep your powder dry.

L—Look before you leap.

M—Much cry, little wool.

N—No vice like avarice.

O—Out of sight, out of mind.

P—Penny-wise, pound-foolish.

Q—Quarrel not with anybody.

R—Rome was not built in a day.

S—Saying and doing are two things.

T—Too much of everything is good for nothing.

U—Union is strength.

V—Vice brings its own punishment.

W—Where there is will, there is a way.

X—X-Ray your own mind.

Y—Your real friend is God only.

Z—Zeal you must have to see God.

Chapter Thirteen

STORIES

HASTE MAKES WASTE

Teacher:—Sohan, Mohan and Vijaya—all of you are here. Very good. Sohan, when did you arrive?

Sohan:—I came this morning, Sir.

Teacher:—What do you want? Should we go on with our story-programme, as usual, this evening also?

Boys:—Yes, Sir.

Teacher:—All right. This time I wish to hear some interesting story from you. How many of you can tell stories? Raise hands.

(All raise their hands)

Wonderful! This shows you are all fond of reading story-books. Then you may take your turns.

(Vijaya raises his hand to take his turn first)

Very well. Vijaya will come forward this time and give us a nice piece of story.

Vijaya:—"A hunter lived in a lonely cottage in a jungle. He had a faithful old hound named Tiger. One day his wife was taken ill. He left his child in the charge of his old dog and went out for hunting. In his absence a wolf stole into the room where the baby lay asleep. He rushed towards the cradle to devour the baby. The dog at once sprang upon the wolf. There was a fierce fight between them. At last the wolf was killed and the faithful dog succeeded in saving the only child of his master. But during the struggle his mouth was besmeared with bloodstains.

When the hunter came back, he met the dog at the door. Seeing his mouth soiled with blood, he thought the dog had probably killed the child. This idea made him mad with rage. He took an aim and shot the dog dead there and then.

On entering the room, he found his child quite safe and a dead wolf lying by his side. He now understood the whole situation. He was very grieved at the loss of his faithful dog who had saved his child at the risk of his own life. He repented and cried; but all his grief and tears could not bring the dog back to life."

Sohan:—Who would not like to possess a faithful dog like Tiger? But fie on the master who suspected the dog's fidelity and shot him dead there and then. What a pity!

Mohan:—Yes, my friend. I quite agree with you. The master was really a big fool. He was so quickly provoked simply on observing the blood-stains on the dog's mouth and lost his wits (Vichara-Sakti). He did not stop to give a moment's thought to study the situation. He did not even enter the cottage to see the things for himself.

Vijaya:—Such passionate, inconsiderate, rash and impatient Asuric type of people are not rare in this world.

Teacher:—Excellent! I have been calmly watching

your reaction and listening to your individual views about the hunter's hasty conduct. I am pleased to know that none of you spoke in favour of the master and all condemned his Satanic and merciless action and his lack of faith in the dog. So, bear in mind, my dear, that *doubt or suspicion is our great enemy. It causes restlessness of mind. Anger and suspicion deprive a man of his reasoning power.*

Do you know what made the master rash, inconsiderate and impatient to act in such a merciless way?

(There was silence for sometime, and none could answer the question.)

It was all due to the master's attachment for the child. It was because of the feeling of extreme love and attachment for his only baby that he was so quickly provoked, grew mad with rage and lost his wits or reason in no time. *In that sudden fit of anger, he could not think aright.*

Do you know the three gates to hell, my boys?

Boys:—No sir. What are they, please?

Sohan:—(In a low tone). Are there any gates to hell also, like those of a king's palace?

(All laugh)

Teacher:—Well, my dear boys, note carefully that lust, anger and greed are the three gates to hell. When a man becomes angry, his mind gets confused. He loses his memory and understanding. In anger he talks anything he likes and does anything he likes. He commits murder. A hot word results in fight and stabbing. An angry man is under intoxication. He loses his senses for the time being. He does not know what he is exactly doing. He is under the sway of anger. Anger destroys the knowledge of the

Self. It is the greatest enemy of peace. All vices, evil qualities and wrong actions take their origin in anger. He who has controlled anger, cannot do anything wrong or evil. Resentment, indignation, fury, irritation are all varieties of anger according to degree or intensity.

Mohan:—Sir, you have described the characteristics of anger in detail, but is there any remedy to get rid of this dire evil?

Teacher:—Well asked, my dear. You seem to be an intelligent boy. I will tell you. Practice of Mouna (silence) and Vichara (right thinking) are of great help in controlling anger. All of a sudden a man gets a terrible fit of anger for trifling matters. If you find it difficult to control anger, leave the place at once and take a brisk walk. Drink some cool water immediately. Anger or irritability is a sign of mental weakness.

When you bring a lighted lamp or torch into a dark room, the darkness vanishes; even so, you can and should control anger or irritability by developing the opposite virtues—patience, Vichara (right thinking or enquiry), love, Kshama (forgiveness) and spirit of service. Then anger will automatically disappear. Hatred ceases not by hatred but by its opposite virtue, 'love', only.

Had the hunter developed in him even a little patience and *Vichara* (right thinking) he would not have lost his faithful dog. You should do nothing in haste. "Haste makes waste", my dear. Think twice before you act. Now you understand, Mohan? Is the whole thing clear to you?

Mohan:—Now I understand, Sir. Having heard the story of "the hunter and the faithful dog" I am reminded of a similar incident that happened with me a few years ago. May I relate the incident here in brief, Sir?

Teacher:—Yes, by all means: Your friends will surely be pleased to hear your experiences in life and will gain thereby.

Mohan:—Once it so happened, Sir, that I bought a beautiful picture of Lord Sri Krishna playing on flute, and placed it on my table by way of decoration. One morning it disappeared from the table. I didn't know who removed it from there. I searched and searched, but all in vain! My younger sister was standing in one corner of the room and was smiling all the time I searched for the picture. I thought that she must have taken away the picture and hidden it somewhere. So, in a fit of anger and suspicion, I began to beat her there and then. She made a lot of hue and cry. Mother rushed to the spot and saved her. She scolded me severely for having beaten my sister whom she thought to be quite innocent. In the afternoon my father returned from his office. Then the whole situation was made clear. The fact was that the room was to be swept of the dust and dirt that day, and my father had removed the Lord's picture from the table, thinking that, during the sweeping process, dust would settle on the picture. So he had put it inside his box and locked it.

Now I realise that I was unduly harsh on my sister who was quite innocent. Had I acted with a little patience and Vichara I would not have handled her so cruelly.

Teacher:—Very nice. Well, my boys, we are getting late now. This evening we had a nice time. You entertained us all with interesting stories and personal experiences. I hope you are amply benefited by today's talks. So, my dear boys, develop positive divine virtues—patience, Vichara (right thinking or enquiry), courage, universal love, spirit of selfless service, strong will, etc. God bless you!

Boys:—Thank you, Sir. We will do as you say. We have changed a lot. All this is due to your grace.

PRIDE GOETH BEFORE A FALL

Teacher:—Hallo, Gopal, this morning you are all in time, I suppose. Where is Krishna?

Gopal:—He is just coming in a few minutes, Sir.

Teacher:—Gopal, can you tell me who the man was with a red turban on his head, yesterday, and what was all that scuffle about?

Gopal:—Yes, Sir. He is my next-door neighbour. He is a very rich man—a millionaire. He is private secretary of *Munim* to our venerable *Seth*, Nemi Chand. He had lent the poor farmer a few hundred rupees and was demanding the amount of interest from him, which the poor farmer could not pay in time, on the fixed date. Hence the trouble arose.

Teacher:—O, I see. He was threatening the farmer and handling him very badly. He boasted of his wealth, name and fame, position and influence. Did you see how proud he was of his possessions? Do you approve of his behaviour?

Gopal:—No, Sir. His behaviour was not at all praiseworthy. We simply condemned the attitude he adopted towards the poor man.

Teacher:—Have you heard the story, "All that glitters is not gold".

Krishna:—Yes, Sir. Perhaps, it is in connection with the proud stag. May I relate the story, Sir?

Teacher:—Yes, proceed.

Krishna:—(Begins) A young stag, as he went over to a spring to quench his thirst, saw himself reflected in the blue water below. He stood still to admire his reflection. He felt proud of his beautiful horns and thought. "Ah, what a splendid pair of horns I have! If the rest of my body were so beautiful, I should have been the most handsome animal alive on earth. But I cannot bear to look at my ugly, thin legs. I am really ashamed of them."

Just then he heard the angry roar of a huge lion, and was off like wind. The legs he had despised, carried him so swiftly that very soon the lion was left far behind. But, as he was going through a thick wood, his splendid horns, that he loved so well, were caught in a bush and he was held captive till the hungry lion came and devoured him.

So, after all, the beautiful horns, which he had admired so much, were the cause of his death.

Teacher:—Very nice. Now you see, boys, how the beautiful horns which the stag was so proud of, brought about his death. Surely, *Pride goeth before a fall*.

As soon as a man gets some power, wealth, name and fame, he is puffed up with vanity and pride. He thinks too much of himself and treats others with contempt. He suffers from superiority-complex and does not like to mix with others.

If any one has some moral qualifications, such as spirit of service or self-sacrifice, he will say, "Who can serve like myself? I am a Brahmachari. I have been practising Brahmacharya for the last ten years" and so on. Just as worldly people are puffed up with the pride of wealth, so also certain Sadhus and religious people boast of their moral qualifications.

Remember, my dear, this kind of pride is a serious obstacle in one's path of material or spiritual progress and brings downfall in the end.

Here I am reminded of an incident from Shivaji's life. It may teach you a good lesson.

Gopal:—What was that incident, Sir? We all are anxious to know about it.

Teacher:—Very well. Listen then.

Once Shivaji engaged thousands of coolies to build a fort. He had the Abhimana or pride that he was feeding all these persons. Shivaji's Guru Swami Ramdas, understood this. He called Shivaji and asked him to break a big stone that was lying in front of his palace. Shivaji ordered a servant to do the work. When the stone was broken, a frog that was inside, jumped out.

Ramdas asked, "O Shivaji! Who has arranged food for this frog that was inside this stone?" Shivaji felt ashamed, prostrated himself before Ramdasji, and said, "O Guru Maharaj! Thou art Antaryamin. Thou hast understood my Abhimana when I thought that these coolies are fed by me. Now Viveka (discrimination) has dawned in me. Protect me, O Lord, I am thy disciple."

So you see, boys, you should not feel proud of your achievements, possessions, wealth and power, name and fame. Remember, wealth and beauty, honour and youth fade away, but the life of righteousness will never decay.

All things are God-given. Nothing belongs to us. We are nobody; we are simply instruments in the Lord's Hands. We should keep up a balanced mind at all times, facing honour and dishonour, prosperity and adversity, heat and cold, pain and pleasure with the same feeling. In adversity we should have patience to bear it, and in prosperity we must not feel proud or elated.

I think we should stop here. This will do for today. This morning we are all in a hurry, you know. God bless you.

Boys:—Thank you very much, Sir.

INDISCRETION HAS ITS TOLLS

(Gopal, Krishna, Rama and other boys come and take their respective seats in the class-room. There is pin-drop silence.)

Krishna:—(Whispers to Gopal). Our Guruji appears to be angry this morning. Don't you notice his frowning looks?

Gopal:—Keep quiet, lest you should fan up his anger.

(All were spellbound, anxious as to who would fall a victim to his angry looks. Nobody ventured to speak.)

Teacher:—Well boys, I am sorry to know that some of you reached home unusually late last night. Here are letters of complaint from your guardians.

(Krishna takes courage and begins.)

Krishna:—May I tell you the fact, Sir, if you don't take it seriously and forgive us?

Teacher:—That is exactly what I expect from you. I want to know plain and simple truth. You should always be bold, honest, truthful and straightforward in whatever you speak or do. Don't be timid.

Krishna:—Very well, Sir. Last evening, as we returned from our usual stroll in the public garden and were passing through a narrow street, a cyclist came from behind. As he rode fast, a little child came in front. To avoid the child, he turned the cycle. A vendor, with a basket full of vegetables, was coming from the opposite direction. The cyclist struck against him. The vendor's basket fell down on the ground and all his things were scattered.

The vendor caught hold of the cyclist and demanded the price of his lost vegetables. A quarrel arose between them. A big crowd of people gathered around them. Some of the acquaintances of the cyclist spoke in his favour while others sided the vendor. From hot words they came to blows. Their clothes were torn and they received bruises and slight injuries on various parts of their bodies.

The police arrived and disengaged them after an effort. The police arrested a few of them. Unfortunately, the policemen, threatening both the parties, accepted bribes from each, with a promise to get the case decided in favour of the party offering a handsome amount. The result was that both the parties had to suffer heavy loss by paying fines and bribing the police.

Teacher:—Did you tell your guardians all about the incident that made you reach home unusually late?

Boys:—Yes Sir. But they doubted our statements.

Teacher:—All right. I shall see to it. Well Gopal, you know why you all come here daily?

Gopal:—Yes, Sir. To learn something new every day.

Teacher:—Right you are. So you should learn some lesson from all such incidents in life. I want to relate a similar story and I hope you will be amply benefited.

(All clap their hands with joy)

Teacher:—(Begins) Once two cats found a loaf of bread. Both fell upon it at the same time. The loaf broke into two pieces. One piece was bigger than the other. They began to quarrel. A monkey passed by at that moment. He said, "Sisters, why are you fighting? What is the matter?" When the cats stated the case, the monkey said: "Do not quarrel. I shall weigh them in a balance for you and make them equal. They both agreed to it. He took a balance and put a piece in each pan. One piece was no doubt heavier than the other. He bit off a piece from the heavier bread and ate it up. Now the other piece became heavier. He bit off a piece from that also and swallowed it. He repeated this process several times until only very small pieces were left behind.

Now the cats realised their folly and requested him to give them back their pieces. But the judge replied: "Do you think I have taken this trouble for nothing? I want my fee as a judge". Saying this, he put the remaining pieces into his mouth and ran away.

Now, my boys, tell me what you learn from this story. Raise hands.

Krishna:—May I speak, Sir.

Teacher:—Yes, go on.

Krishna:—Sir, we should settle our affairs amongst ourselves, if there be any.

Teacher:—Perfectly correct. You are a very clever boy. Is it not?

Gopal:—Sir, we should not allow a third party to interfere.

Teacher:—Very nice. You have completed the answer. So you see, my boys, "Indiscretion has its tolls."

Now, then, it is time for us to disperse. Wish you all good luck.

Boys:—Thank you very much, Sir.

SELFISHNESS AND MEAN-MINDEDNESS LEAD TO SUFFERING

Teacher:—O Mohan, you have come! Where had you been for the last four days?

Mohan:—Sir, I returned only this morning from Amritsar where I had gone to join my sister's marriage.

Teacher:—How is it that you appear dull and sleepy? Have you been unwell?

Mohan:—No, Sir. I had to keep awake the whole night because of the great rush of passengers in the third class compartment; otherwise the journey was quite enjoyable. I could not get a wink of sleep.

Gopal:—Sir, Mohan says that he experienced a very interesting incident during his return journey from Amritsar. We are eager to hear him.

Teacher:—Well, Mohan, your classmates are very

desirous to know of your experiences. Will you like to oblige them?

Mohan:—Certainly, Sir. I am always at their service (Begins).

At Amritsar station, when the train arrived at the platform, the third-class compartments were awfully packed with passengers. Somehow we got into the compartment. One passenger had occupied one full berth and stretched himself at full length. Two strong and sturdy Pathans were also standing beside the door of the compartment. They requested the gentleman to get up and make room for others. He turned a deaf ear to their request. Once again the Pathans asked the man to make his fellow-passengers comfortable, but he indifferently murmured: "I am bound on a long journey, so I must have enough space to stretch my legs." The Pathans said: "You have no right to make yourself comfortable at others' cost." Saying this, they both stood, one on each side of the sleeping man. He was bodily lifted and put down on the floor of the compartment. He frowned terribly and cast angry looks at the Pathans and clenched his fist but could do nothing. All the other passengers kept mum, but laughed in their sleeves and enjoyed the fun. The Pathans took their seats with two other passengers, on the berth.

(All the boys had a hearty laugh)

Teacher:—Well, boys, you seem to enjoy the talk very much. I give you four words—"mean-mindedness, selfishness, obstinacy, haughtiness." Try to pick out a suitable word that can be very well used to describe this type of man. I allow you two minutes to think over.

Krishna:—Sir, in my opinion, the man was extremely selfish.

Gopal:—Sir, he was not only selfish but mean-minded also. It is quite evident that he was at fault. So, instead of admitting his mistake, he frowned and grew furious. This shows his mean mentality.

Mohan:—Sir, I agree with my friend, Gopal; but besides being selfish and mean-minded, he was haughty also, because he asserted his right to occupy the full berth and justified his evil conduct.

Sohan:—Sir, I think there is no use of giving any more explanations. To sum up, he was a good mixture of all these evil qualities. He did not get up in spite of repeated requests from the Pathans. So he was obstinate also.

Teacher:—Very nice. My dear boys, I am very much pleased to see that you exerted your brains to your utmost. You all deserve credit for that and all are correct, more or less. I hope you would welcome another story from me in brief, which may make the point clearer still.

All boys:— Yes, Sir. You are quite welcome with your story. We shall be too pleased to have it.

Teacher:—Very well. Listen then.

There was an old wicked dog. He jumped into a manger full of dry hay and barked at any one who came near. He would not let the cattle eat hay, nor could he eat the hay himself. One day an ox came to eat the grass, but the dog jumped at him and barked him off. The ox said: "Why do you prevent me from eating hay which is of no use to you?" The dog replied: "Since I cannot eat it, no one else shall eat it." The poor ox went away.

One day a donkey saw the manger full of nice dry hay. His mouth began to water. He approached the manger and stole a mouthful. The dog growled at him and tried to bite him. But the donkey turned round and kicked and kicked. The dog received a hard kick on his mouth and ran off whining painfully all the way. The donkey ate the hay to his heart's content and left the rest for the ox.

Now, boys, just revise both the incidents in your minds. You may arrive at some definite conclusions.

Gopal:—Now the whole thing is clear to me, Sir. The dog would not let the cattle eat hay, nor could he eat it himself. This is clear. mean-mindedness and worse than selfishness.

Teacher:—So you see, boys, selfishness degenerates into mean-mindedness. This world abounds in mean-minded people of every sort. The heart of a mean-minded man burns when he sees others in prosperous condition. He will eat sweetmeats, fruits, etc., but his heart will burn if his servant also eats the same articles. He will make great differences in serving tea or anything to others. He will keep the best thing for himself and distribute the rotten stuff to others. A mean-minded man will not hesitate to poison his brother to usurp his property. He will not hesitate to utter lies, defraud a man and rob him of his wealth. He is ready to do any kind of mean act to amass wealth. He may be a great man in society but he will be shamelessly fighting on the railway platform with a porter for two paise. He will not give even a single morsel of food to save a dying man. He has a heart as hard as stone. Charity is unknown to him.

Do you know its opposite virtue which everyone should cultivate?

Mohan:—Yes, Sir. You gave us the names of so many positive virtues in previous talks. In this case, the opposite virtue is, in my opinion, nobility or generosity, charitable nature or universal love.

Teacher:—Wonderful! You are growing wiser day by day. All right. This will do for today. Let us disperse now for lunch. God bless you all.

Boys:—Thank you so much, Sir.

TEMPTATION INVOLVES ONE IN TROUBLE

Teacher:—Sohan, why do you look so gloomy today? Oh! I see tears streaming down your cheeks. What makes you so unhappy? Go to the adjoining bathroom, wipe off your tears, wash your face, make yourself calm and then tell me what has made you so miserable. I shall see if I can be of any help to you.

(Sohan goes to the bathroom and returns after five minutes).

Oh! You have come. Now tell me what is wrong with you.

Sohan:—Sir, this morning, some of my friends took me along with them to the fruits-garden nearby. The owner of the garden was not there. We all began to pluck mangoes and eat them. Some filled their pockets with the ripe fruits. Soon after, we saw the gardener coming at a distance. All my friends took to their heels, but the gardener caught hold of me, pulled me by the ears, slapped me badly and turned me out.

Teacher:—Very sorry to hear all this. But I am glad that you have spoken the truth and told me everything without any reserve. I understand; so you fell a prey to the mischief played by your naughty friends. They ran off leaving you behind alone, to be beaten and insulted by the gardener. Still, it is a surprise to me that you, a good boy as you are, were tempted to accompany them. Is it a public garden where everybody can go and enjoy the fruits, freely?

Sohan:— No Sir, it is a private garden and none is allowed there. We entered by the back door.

Teacher:—Entering the garden stealthily by the back-door! Didn't you do something very objectionable?

Sohan:—All entered the same way, Sir.

Teacher:—If all your friends fall into the well, will you also follow their example?

Sohan:—No Sir, I am really ashamed of myself.

Teacher:—Very good. Then you realise your mistake. If you were all so eager to eat mangoes, you could have waited and taken permission of the gardener. Perhaps you were so much overpowered by temptation that you could not stop a while to think of your undesirable act and the consequences thereof. However, don't worry. "To err is human; to forgive is divine". Take courage. It is all well, if this incident in your life teaches you some useful lesson. Now you realise, my dear, how temptation involves one in trouble. "Think twice before you leap." You took a leap in the dark. Didn't you?

Sohan:—Yes Sir, I do realise my mistake. They forced me to accompany them and I had to go much against my will. Inside the garden also I warned my friends not to touch the fruits without permission but they would not heed my warning.

Teacher:—Do you know the story of the rotten apples, my dear?

Sohan:—No Sir. Anyway, I would like to hear it because I know that the stories you tell, are always interesting and instructive.

Teacher:—Very well. Then hear me attentively.

"Ahmed was a good boy. He always obeyed his parents. One of his playmates was a very wicked boy. He was a perfect loafer and always neglected his school-work. He wasted much of time and money. Ahmed soon got into the bad company of that boy.

Ahmed's father came to know of it. He made up his mind to save his son from the bad company. At last he hit upon a nice plan. One day he gave him some good apples and told him to lay them aside for a few days.

The same night the father placed a rotten-apple among the good ones. Two days after he asked his son to fetch the apples. To his surprise, he found all the apples quite rotten. He asked his father about it. The father explained to him how one rotten apple had spoiled the good ones. He then advised him to shun the company of that bad boy, or he, too, would be spoiled. Henceforward, Ahmed gave up the company of that bad boy."

Now you see, my dear Sohan, how one rotten apple spoiled the other good ones. You understand the harm done by bad company. So, be very *vigilant* and shun the company of your bad friends. Otherwise, you will also be spoiled.

You have yet to experience a lot of "ups and downs" in life. The so-called friends are your real enemies. You cannot find even a single unselfish friend in this world. Worldly friends come to you to get money and other comforts, when you have got plenty of them. When you are in adverse circumstances, no one will care to look at you. This world is full of avarice, hypocrisy, double dealing, flattery, untruth, cheating and selfishness. You have to be very careful, my boy. Friends come to have idle talk with you and waste your time. They will say, "Friend, what are you doing? Earn money as much as possible, by any means. Live comfortably now. Eat, drink, and be merry. Let us go to talkies. Today there is a good new American Hollywood production running at so and so theatre. There is a beautiful American dance. Who knows about the future? Where is God? Where is heaven? There is nothing beyond this world." All these are fair-weather friends. You will get such sorts of advice from such worldly friends. Whereas, they will desert you in adverse circumstances. In case you marry, even your would-be wife and sons may forsake you after some time.

Sohan:—Sir, certainly, it is very kind of you to have warned me in time. "Forewarned is forearmed." I shall always be on my guard. But will you tell me how to avoid these evils, Sir?

Teacher:—I am pleased to see that you are so inquisitive to know more about life. Life is not all a bed of roses. You have to do a lot of selection and rejection work. You will have to cast off many evil traits—selfishness, lust, anger, greed, hatred and jealousy and retain and develop only what is good, i.e., various virtues such as, mercy, forgiveness, universal love, tolerance, patience, courage, strong will, etc.

So the best way my dear, is to cut off all connections with your friends. Don't talk to any of them, however sincere they may seem to be. It is better to live alone than in bad company. Trust in that *only Immortal Friend*, then alone you are perfectly safe. He will give you whatever you want. Hear His sweet counsel from within, with one-pointed mind, and follow it.

Sohan:—Who is that Immortal Friend, Sir? I don't quite follow you.

Teacher:—That Immortal Friend, your real friend in need, who attends on you sincerely and who dwells in your heart, is your Supreme Self, the All-pervading God.

Sohan:—You have removed most of my doubts, and given me very useful instructions. Thank you, Sir.

Teacher:—God bless you.

RETURN GOOD FOR EVIL

Teacher:—Hallo, Master Ajay! Why are you all so late this morning?

Ajay:—A magician was showing a few tricks by the wayside. We all stopped to enjoy the fun for a while, Sir.

Teacher:—No matter, let us begin, then.

Sohan:—This morning, it is my turn to tell a story, Sir.

Teacher:—All right. Are you well prepared? Let me see how you entertain your friends this morning.

Sohan:—Once a rich farmer was standing at his door. A beggar went to him and asked him for something to eat and drink. The farmer abused him and turned him out.

After some days the farmer went out for hunting. The night came on and he lost his way. He came to a hut. He went there and asked for food and shelter. The owner of the hut was a very poor man, but he gave him food to eat and a bed to sleep in.

Early next morning the poor man woke the farmer and showed him his way out of the forest. In the day-light the farmer recognised him. He was the same beggar whom he had turned away from his door. The farmer hung down his head in shame and begged his pardon saying: "You have taught me a lesson by returning good for evil. I shall never refuse food to a beggar again."

Ajay:—Sir, the farmer committed a grave sin. Instead of giving the beggar something as charity, he abused him and turned him out. He insulted the poor beggar and injured his feelings. It was a grave sin. There is no doubt about it.

Mohan:—It was the height of folly. His conduct shows how proud he was of his wealth and position. Had the beggar abused him in return, it would have surely touched the rich man's feelings of pride and superiority. He could not have borne the insult and would have come to blows with the beggar.

Sohan:—On the contrary, look at the generosity of the beggar, my friends. How patiently and calmly he bore the insult and injury done to him! He did not utter a single word, and went his way as if nothing had happened.

He strictly followed the principle: "Bear insult, bear injury,—the highest Sadhana". He did not seem to be an ordinary beggar, but spiritually he was a highly advanced sage, his very behaviour showed his divine qualities and the most noble traits in his character. He gave the farmer food and shelter when he lost his way in the jungle at night. He entirely forgot all about the bad turn the rich man had done to him a few days ago. He never retaliated, though he had a good chance to avenge himself. He was so generous, charitable and hospitable.

Vijaya:—My friends, you all condemn the farmer's conduct and praise the beggar for his generosity. So, according to your viewpoint, the wicked farmer ought to have been punished for the wrong he had done. Had I been in place of the beggar, I would have taught the farmer a nice lesson and brought him to his senses.

Mohan:—What lesson would you have taught him,—may I know?

Vijaya:—I would have starved him for the whole night and in the morning, let my dog loose to chase him out of the forest. That would have been the best way to bring him to his senses.

Mohan:—Is this all that you have been learning from our respected teacher, so far? Is this a divine way of doing things? Is this the golden rule *(Return good for evil)* that Guruji has been teaching us all along? If a wicked person sticks to his wickedness, why should not a good man adhere to his righteous conduct? We are not going to follow bad examples and give up goodness. Don't you remember that our Guruji taught us: "Return love for hatred. If you are not able to do that, be indifferent. But never meet hatred with hatred."

Teacher:—Very good Mohan. Your arguments are really praiseworthy. Don't you notice, boys, the reaction of the beggar's hospitality on the rich farmer; how the latter was ashamed and asked the beggar to pardon him? Not only this; he actually promised that he would never refuse food to a beggar again. This charitable behaviour in return, was in itself a punishment to the rich man. One should conquer hatred by love.

The beggar by his kind hospitality, by helping the rich farmer out of his difficulty, by returning good for evil, lowered and curbed the farmer's pride. What a nice way of reforming a proud man! This is the right way to make a man realise his mistake, not by letting the dogs loose after him in a revengeful spirit. That way you will only be fanning the fire of anger, hatred and enmity. I think there are still some doubts in your minds regarding your behaviour towards others under circumstances as these. Should I give you another set of instructions in this connection?

Mohan:—Yes Sir, they will definitely be of great value to us all, for our future guidance.

Teacher:—Very well. Then note down and preserve these carefully:—

1. Do all the good that you can, in all the ways you can, to all people you can, at all times, with all zeal, strength and love.

2. Let mercy soften your heart. Let virtue gladden your heart. Let continence purify your heart.

3. Practise non-injury, my dear boys. If you injure any other creature, you really injure yourself, because God that dwells in you, dwells in all. Only one Soul dwells in all beings. Therefore love all as your own self.

Are these instructions enough, or do you want more?

Boys:—These instructions are simply inspiring, Sir. Let us have more, if you can give.

Teacher:—Very well. Can you name some most familiar flowers you know?

Mohan:—Yes Sir, why not?
Lily, Rose, Queen of the night, Lotus, Jasmine.

Teacher:—Very nice. That will do. Now take down.

4. In the garden of your heart, plant the lily of love, the rose of purity, the 'queen-of-the-night' of compassion, the lotus of courage and jasmine of humility.

(All laugh heartily)

Boys:—This instruction (i.e., gardening of the heart with flowers of divine virtues) is the best and most enjoyable, Sir, which we can never forget.

Teacher:—I am extremely happy to find that you are so much interested in moral and spiritual discourses.

5. Humility and forgiveness are the highest of all virtues. God helps you only when you become utterly humble. Remember, my dear, humility is not cowardice, as many people think. Meekness is not weakness. Humility and meekness are indeed spiritual powers.

6. He who shows courtesy reaps friendship; he who plants kindness reaps love.

7. Anger is the worst fire. Lust is an all-consuming

Mohan:—No Sir, he must compensate the loss or suffer punishment unconditionally. I won't spare him under any condition.

Teacher:—Suppose, for a moment, you, perchance, break his watch unintentionally, of course, would you like to be punished or to bear the heavy cost?

Mohan:—No Sir, because I did not do it intentionally.

Teacher:—Then why do you impose such hard conditions on your friend? Do to others as you wish to be done by. Follow the golden rule, "If evil or wrong is done unto you, return thou good again." Don't try to retaliate, but forgive. Be charitable, large-hearted, generous and broad-minded. You should develop these virtues which are divine in nature. Now you understand how you should behave under circumstances as these, my dear.

What will you do if somebody abuses you? Will you pay him in the same coin?

Mohan:—No, never, I won't mind it, and will remain indifferent, because just now, you instructed me not to retaliate, but be good and do good in turn.

Teacher:—Very nice, that is something praiseworthy. Do you want to become divine or devilish? What do you want to become, a Rama or a Ravana?

Mohan:—I would like to become a Rama, to be sure.

Teacher:—Wonderful! You know, my dear, *love begets love, and hatred begets hatred*. If you love others, all will love you. If you develop the aforesaid divine virtues, you will grow into an ideal boy. God will love you and you will have all success.

Do you know the *Three Rules?*

Mohan:—No Sir, what are those rules? Will you kindly tell me? I shall try to follow them.

Teacher:—Very good, you are an intelligent boy.

Hear then:—

A.   What is the iron rule?
        The rule of savage men—
        If good is done unto thee,
        Return thou evil again:
        This is the iron rule.

B.   What is the silver rule?
        The rule of worldly men—
        If evil is done unto thee,
        Return thou evil again:
        This is the silver rule.

C.   What is the Golden Rule?
        The rule of righteous me —
        If evil is done unto thee,
        Return thou good again:
        This is the Golden Rule.

Now, my dear Mohan, tell me what rule you will follow and stick to?

Mohan:—I want to follow the last, the Golden Rule, Sir.

Teacher:—Wonderful. That is a very good choice. God bless you.

Mohan:—Thank you, Sir.

KINDNESS BRINGS ITS OWN REWARD

Teacher:—Hallo! Master Gopal, you look quite fresh, and glorious in your new dress this morning. Come and sit down here. I want to tell you something new today. What is Ethics? Do you know?

Gopal:—This is the first time I have heard this word. It is all Greek and Latin to me. I would request you to explain it in detail, Sir.

Teacher:—Doesn't matter. I will make it clear to you just now. Ethics is the science of right conduct. Ethical science shows the way in which human beings should behave towards one another and towards other creatures. It contains systematised principles on which man should act. Without Ethics you cannot have any progress in this world or in the spiritual path. Ethics is morality. He who leads a perfect moral life, attains to everlasting happiness. Practice of Ethics will help you to live in harmony with your neighbours, friends, your own family- members, fellow-beings and all other people.

Krishna:—What is right conduct, Sir, may I know? It is not quite clear.

Teacher:—Well asked. I shall tell you. That act which does not do good to others, or that act for which one has to repent or feel shame later on, should never be done. That act, on the other hand, should be done, for which one may be praised in society. You should do such acts as are praiseworthy and which bring good to you and to others. This is a brief description of what right conduct is.

Gopal:—We have been hearing these words frequently—conduct, character and Sadachara. They are a bit confusing. Do they all mean one and the same thing, Sir?

Teacher:—Oh, you are bombarding me with question after question.

Gopal:—You are a mine of knowledge, Sir.

Teacher:—So, you mean to blow it up, so that nothing is left there.

(All burst forth into hearty laughter)

Anyway, I must satisfy you and clear your doubts.

Conduct is one's personal behaviour towards others in daily life. The sum total of one's virtues forms one's character. It is character that gives real force and power to man. They say, "Knowledge is power", but I say, with all the emphasis at my command, that "Character is power". Without character the attainment of knowledge is impossible. The man who has no character, is practically a dead man in this world. He is ignored and despised by the community. If you want success in life, if you want to influence others, if you want to progress in the world and in the spiritual path, you must possess a spotless character. Sankara, Buddha, Jesus and other Rishis of yore are remembered even now, because they had wonderful character. They influenced people and converted others through their force of character. Character is life's pillar. Character expresses itself as conduct or we may say: "One's daily conduct reveals one's character."

That aspect of ethical science which treats of the modes of right conduct, moral living and performance of duty, is Sadachara.

To speak the truth, to practise Ahimsa, not to hurt the feelings of others in thought, word and deed, not to speak harsh words to anyone, not to show anger towards anybody, not to abuse or speak ill of others and to see God in all beings, is Sadachara.

Rama:—Sir, character is a mighty soul-force, then.

Teacher:—Yes, my dear, it is like a sweet flower that spreads its fragrance far and wide. A man of noble traits and good character possesses a tremendous personality. A man may be a skilful artist. He may be a clever musician, he may be an able poet or a great scientist. But if he has no character, he can have no real position in society. People will despise him. In a broad sense, a man of character is expected to be kind, merciful, truthful, forgiving and tolerant. He is expected to possess all the virtues.

But if he speaks deliberate untruth, if he is selfish and greedy, if he hurts the feelings of others, he is called a man of bad character. One should try to develop a perfect and spotless character.

Gopal:—What are the qualifications of a man of perfect and spotless character, Sir?

Teacher:—Your questions are very trying. Isn't it? A man of spotless character should possess the following virtues. I am afraid you will be tired of hearing them, so numerous they are. I give you a few important qualifications only, such as, humility, non-injury in thought, word and deed, fearlessness, charity, strong will, modesty, self-control, absence of anger or wrath, envy or pride, purity and compassion to all living beings.

Can you tell, Rama, why one should not kill or injure others; why one should love one's neighbour?

Rama:—Just a minute, please, and I shall try to answer the question, Sir,......

(Thinks for a while, and then says)

"Because God is one and all beings are but His manifestations or creation; there is One Self in all, so, if we injure others, we injure our own Self."

Teacher:—Wonderful. Exactly so; you seem to be an intelligent boy.

Gopal:—A little time is left for the story, Sir, may I begin one?

Teacher:—Very good, you have reminded me in time. All right, proceed on.

Gopal:—(Begins) Once a master used to treat his slave, named Androcles, very badly. He beat him with a whip for the slightest fault. Moreover, he was half-starved. The slave was so much tired of his life that one day he ran away into the jungle.

He heard a painful cry from some bushes. He went towards it. He saw there a lion groaning. The lion was holding up and showing him his paw. A big thorn had run into his paw. The slave went near and took the thorn out. He then bound the wound with a piece of cloth. The lion felt relief. He lay at Androcle's feet, began to wag his tail and lick his hands like a pet dog. They became friends and began to live together in the same cave.

A few months later, the slave was caught by his master's men. He was taken before the king who ordered that the slave should be thrown before a hungry lion. The day was fixed. Thousands of people came to see the spectacle of the fight between the lion and the slave, Androcles. The poor slave was put in an enclosure. A hungry lion was let in. The lion roared terribly and rushed towards him. But reaching near the slave, the lion recognised the man who was his old friend. The lion at once fell down at his feet, licked his hand and wagged his tail. At this strange sight, the king and all his courtiers were filled with astonishment.

The king called the slave, Androcles, to him. The slave related the whole story of their friendship. Hearing it the king was so pleased that he set both the slave and the lion at liberty.

Teacher:—It is a very interesting and instructive story. So you see, my boys, "Kindness brings its own reward." Do you know the story of "The kind girl"?

Boys:—No, Sir. You have excited our curiosity to hear it. It must be as entertaining as that of "the slave and the lion".

Teacher:—A railway train was passing through a jungle. It was evening. There were green fields on both sides of the railway line. Many men, women and children were working in the fields. A girl was grazing the cattle near the river-bridge.

It rained heavily that day. The water in the river rose high. It cut down the banks. The bridge of the river was old. It was broken on one side. The sandy bank was washed away. The girl knew it. It was the time when a railway train came. The train had to cross the bridge. The girl thought that many lives would be lost. How could she stop the engine? Suddenly a thought came into her mind.

The train was running fast. No time was to be lost. She took off her red sari. She ran to the bank where the bridge was broken. She began to wave her Sari above her head.

The driver saw the red signal. The train had already crossed half the bridge. It was with great difficulty that the driver stopped the engine. The driver saw the danger. The guard also came there. All understood what the danger was. Lives of hundreds of people were saved.

Krishna:—Wonderful! She was really a brave girl. She did the noblest deed.

Gopal:—The girl was a true heroine indeed. She was gifted with courage and feeling of universal love.

Teacher:—So you see, boys, little acts of kindness, little acts of courtesy purify our hearts and make us more and more God-conscious.

Rama:—Sir, my mind is filled with the thought of "the master and the slave, Androcles".

Why did the master treat the slave so mercilessly? He could have dismissed him from service.

Teacher:—There was a time, my dear, when men and women also were sold as slaves like animals. Rich men kept them not as servants but as slaves and treated them cruelly if they failed to satisfy their masters with their work. The masters got angry at the slightest wrong done by the slaves. They were bound to work as lifelong slaves. If they ran away, they were chased, caught and punished heavily, because they were bought by rich men and were considered as their personal property.

Gopal:—It was really very cruel and shameful of the

masters to behave towards the poor slaves like that. How could Androcles venture to go near the lion, Sir?

Teacher:—The lion was piteously groaning with pain and showing his paw to Androcles who could clearly see a thorn in the lion's paw. Besides this, the lion looked gentle and moved the heart of the slave with pity. So the slave gathered courage, held the lion's paw in his hands, and pulled out the big thorn. The lion was relieved of its pain and began to wag his tail out of gratitude.

Krishna:—How could the ferocious lion be so kind to the slave Sir?

Teacher:—Animals are also very sensitive. They respond to the nature of treatment they receive from others. That is why most of the ferocious animals like elephants, tigers, dogs and others can be tamed and trained as well.

Krishna:—Sir, it excites a curiosity in me to know about them and their work.

Teacher:—Yes, my dear, it is something worth knowing.

St. Bernard dogs are trained to find and save people lost in the snow on the Alps, in Switzerland. Red Cross dogs help ambulance parties in battles. Every Red Cross dog has bandages and dressings strapped to his collar and often a small bottle of brandy also. When the dog finds a wounded man who can help himself a little, it will stand while the man takes dressings and bandages to tie up his wounds with. If the man is so badly wounded that he cannot help himself, the dog will stand by and bark. The stretcher-bearers will hear the barking, come and carry away the poor man to a first-aid station behind the battle-field.

Krishna:—It is simply wonderful and surprising that dogs can also do such humanitarian work!

Gopal:—This morning, we had a long and most entertaining talk, Sir. We are sorry to have detained you for so long this time, and troubled you with a volley of questions.

Teacher:—Never mind. It is a great pleasure to me to answer all your curious enquiries. I am glad to have students of inquisitive nature, like you all. God bless you.

Boys:—Thank you very much, Sir.

REGULARITY AND PUNCTUALITY—TWO KEYS TO SUCCESS IN ALL WALKS OF LIFE

(Rama and Krishna are talking to each other in the classroom.)

Rama:—Hallo Krishna! the examination is now fast approaching. I have completed my preparations for it. How much work you have done?

Krishna:—I have done nothing so far. I have been enjoying games and play.

Rama:—How would you pass the examination without preparation? May I know that?

Krishna:— I have a mind not to appear for the examination this year.

Rama:—I am sorry to hear of your strange resolve, my friend.

(Teacher enters)

Teacher:—Why do you look so very dejected this morning, Krishna?

Rama:—Sir, he does not intend to sit for the examination this time. He says that he has been very irregular in his studies. He has been enjoying games and play and has done nothing so far.

Teacher:—Is it so, my boy? Remember, it is never too late. There are yet two months for the examination. If you begin to work from today, you can make up for your deficiency. A little work, done regularly, will enable you to pass the examination. Duty is hard, but its fruit is sweet. You should never shirk duty for the sake of pleasure and games.

So, don't worry. Cheer up, my boy. Take courage. Be up and doing. Give up this idea of absenting yourself from the examination, and gird up your loins to work hard. The man who is regular and punctual will get sure success in all walks of life. Have you not heard of the story of Damon and Pythias?

Boys:—No, Sir.

Teacher:—Oh, it is a wonderful incident. It will give you a clear idea as to what *Punctuality* can do or achieve.

Damon and Pythias were fast friends in Syracuse (Italy). Pythias committed some crime and was condemned to death by the king. He requested for permission to visit his family and promised to return on the day of execution. His fast friend Damon offered himself as surety. The day of execution arrived but Pythias was not to be seen. Damon prepared himself to die. He was taken to the scaffold. The people, gathered there, shed tears for Damon who was quite innocent, and was a sincere friend. There was perfect gloom pervading all over the place.

Just then, out of the stillness, came the sound of the clattering of the horse's hoofs and a loud voice resounded through the air: "Stop, stop the execution". The people cheered loudly as Damon was ordered to leave the scaffold. But Damon, having no family, insisted on dying for his friend. Pythias did not agree to it. The king was so much impressed by their friendship that he cancelled the order of death, and himself became their friend.

So, you see boys, had Pythias been a minute late, Damon would have been dead. The one important virtue that gives sure success in life is *Punctuality*.

Krishna:—Sir, your talk has made me wiser than I was before. You have saved me from the wrong path that would have led me to utter ruin. I promise to abide by your advice and hope to work hard henceforth. I thank you for your good advice Sir.

Teacher:—God bless you, my boy. The man who is irregular and does his work by fits and starts cannot reap the fruits of his efforts. Regularity, punctuality and discipline go hand in hand. College and school students in India imitate the West in fashion, style, cropping the hair, etc. These are all vile imitations. We should imbibe from them the important virtues, such as, punctuality and regularity. See how an Englishman adjusts his time to the very second! How punctual he is! They are more studious, regular and punctual than the Indians. The number of specialists and research scholars is larger in the West than in India.

Learn your lessons from Nature. Mark how the season rotates regularly! Mark how the sun rises and sets, how the monsoon comes, how the flowers blossom, how the fruits and vegetables grow, how the revolution of the moon and the earth takes place, how the days and nights, weeks and months and years roll on! Nature is our Guru and Guide.

Have regular habits in all walks of life. Be regular in going to bed and in getting up early in the morning. "Early to bed and early to rise makes one healthy, wealthy and wise." Be very regular in your meals always, in your studies, in your physical exercises, in your prayers and meditation, etc. You will have a very successful life, and a happy one, too. Regularity and punctuality should be your watchword.

MANNERS AND CLEANLINESS IMPRESS EVERYONE

(Mohan, the class monitor, comes to the office to report that too much noise and disturbance is going on in the class. The bell rings and the teacher enters the class).

Teacher:—Well boys, the monitor reports that you indulged freely in creating unpleasantness, breaking the class-discipline and in behaving in a discourteous manner. It is something very undesirable. This sort of conduct is never expected from such advanced students as you are.

However, let us go through our usual programme first, and then I shall take up the matter, if necessary. This morning I am going to tell you a story from which you will learn how you should behave and what good habits you should develop.

A gentleman once advertised for a young clerk to help him in his office. About fifty young men applied for the post. Many had long testimonials and strong recommendations. The gentleman selected one who had no recommendation and sent the rest away. A friend who sat beside him said, "I should like to know for what reason you chose that boy. He had no testimonials or recommendations."

"You are mistaken", said the gentleman, "he had a great many. He wiped his feet when he entered the room and closed the door after him. This shows he was tidy and orderly."

"He lifted up the book which I had purposely placed on the floor, and placed it on the table, while others had just stepped over it. He gave up his seat to that old lame man. This shows that he was gentle and courteous. His clothes were carefully brushed and his hair in order. He had a neat and dignified appearance. He waited quietly for his turn, while others pushed each other aside. This shows he has good manners."

"Don't you call these recommendations? I do, so I have employed this young man. I think I have made the right choice."

Mohan, you personally witnessed the disturbances that took place in the class. Would you tell me who were responsible for them?

Mohan:—Yes, Sir; Sohan quarrelled with his friend to occupy the front seat and both behaved discourteously towards each other. A few books were thrown down on the floor. Some boys stepped over the books. Vijaya and Sohan were pushing each other and shouting unnecessarily.

Teacher:—So, their conduct was just the reverse of

that of the candidate mentioned in the story. Well, boys, I am sorry to hear all about your behaviour from the monitor.

Your faces are advertisement boards showing all your inner thoughts. Just compare your conduct with that of the successful candidate in the story. Look within, find out your own faults and weaknesses, see where you stand, and then try to mend yourselves.

Just mark, boys, out of fifty applicants with strong recommendations, only one, who had no recommendation, was chosen. Why?

Gopal:—Because he was neat and well-mannered, Sir. He was tidy and orderly, gentle and courteous.

Teacher:—You are right. He possessed all these virtues which served him as real recommendations, on the strength of which he superseded all others, and won the job. Now tell me, boys, what qualifications you possess, and what reward you expect from me for the conduct you showed in the class this morning.

Boys:—We are ashamed for our conduct, Sir. This is enough. Kindly don't put us to shame any more. We assure you that, in future, you won't hear any complaint against us.

Teacher:—I have every reason to trust you, because there is no virtue greater than sincerity, and sincere repentance means a lot. A sincere man is very soft-hearted, frank and honest, true and free from hypocrisy. People place full faith in his words and are quite eager to take him in their service.

But take this as a word of caution and warning from

me. This is the age of scientific inventions, the age of fashion and false notions. People are acting according to their own whims and fancies. Evil habits of all sorts have cropped up in all, even in so-called civilised societies. For example, a friend greets another friend not with the names of God, "Jai Sri Krishna", "Om Namo Narayanaya", but with a packet of cigarettes. He says, "Come along, Mr. Joshi, have a smoke, have a drink, a peg of whisky", and so on.

Bear in mind, boys, alcohol is such a bad devil that, if once it enters the system of man, it never leaves him till he becomes a confirmed drunkard. Alcohol is a deadly poison that destroys the brain-cells, and nerves.

Another evil habit is smoking which is so very common all the world over. Habitual smokers bring very clever arguments to support their case. They say, "Smoking keeps the bowels clean. I get a good motion in the morning." Smoking, beware my boys, brings nicotine poisoning of the whole system.

Then the other evil habits are betel-chewing, drinking strong tea, coffee, etc.

Mohan:—Drinking tea or coffee is not a bad habit, Sir. Everybody takes tea nowadays.

Teacher:—Yes, you are right there. In happy moderation, tea or coffee helps hard-workers. But the thing is that man loses his will-power and finds it hard to resist falling into immoderation. There comes the whole trouble. He becomes a slave to these drinks. If he can remain as a master and can give it up at any time, there is no harm.

The vast majority of persons have got the evil habit of using vulgar words always, during their conversation, specially when they become excited and angry. A man of refined taste, culture and polish can never utter any such words. So my dear, always shun bad company,—of smokers, drinkers and vulgar people. There is nothing really impossible under the sun. Where there is a will, there is a way.

Very well, now let us disperse. May God give you strength and will-power enough to keep yourselves aloof from all these bad habits.

Boys:—Thank you very much, Sir.

TRUST IN GOD AND DO THE RIGHT

Teacher:—Mohan, why are you so late? Sight-seeing?

Boys:—No Sir. It is with great difficulty and gentle persuasions that we could bring Sohan to school this morning. Hence the delay.

Teacher:—What happened to him?

Mohan:—Sir, he got plucked in the Hindi Bhushan examination. So he curses God and his fate. He neither eats nor drinks, neither sleeps nor rests, but weeps day in and day out, and behaves like a mad man. His parents are very much worried on his account.

Teacher:—Where is he? Bring him to me. (*Two boys fetch Sohan to the class*). Sohan, look at me, why do you feel so much worried, simply because you failed in the examination and received a slight setback in the battle of life?

Sohan:—(Wiping off his tears) Sir, I had high hopes.

I spared no pains, worked hard and burnt the midnight oil, to pass this examination, but, as ill-luck would have it, all my hopes were turned to dust and all my efforts came to nothing. Now, what should I do but to curse my fate?

Teacher:—Well, my boy, don't be silly. It is not becoming of a man of nerves to lose heart and lament like this in the face of trials and difficulties. God is great, and mysterious are his ways. He is all-merciful. Did you pray to God during the period of your earnest preparations for the examination? Did you crave for the Lord's blessings? It is because we forget and eliminate God from our daily activities in life that pain, sorrow and all sorts of sufferings come to us, in this world, to curb our ego. As a matter of fact, all these sufferings are blessings in disguise. They are the gifts of God for our purification. The adversities that come to us have a great purpose and a meaning in them. You know the proverb, "To come out pure gold, character must pass through the furnace of afflictions."

Sohan:—How can we know, Sir, that these difficulties and troubles have some purpose and meaning behind them, simply because you tell us we should accept them as such.

Teacher:—Very good. It is an intelligent question, my boy. Suppose a man has developed a boil on some part of his body. It is full of pus and he experiences great pain.

The doctor takes up a sharp knife and wants to open it to remove the pus—the real cause of pain. The man, through his ignorance, of course, can think that the doctor is going to kill him or injure him. Really speaking, the doctor is his well-wisher, and wants to relieve him of his suffering, by operating upon the boil.

Even so, through our ignorance, we hold God responsible for all our troubles and failures that come to us in life, and foolishly begin to curse Him. Ignorance is the source of all sins. You badly need a Divine dose, my dear.

It was in quest of this Divine dose (i.e. Enlightenment) that Gautama Buddha bade good-bye to his parents, his beloved wife and child, and all the comforts and luxuries of the royal palace. The Divine or Spiritual Dose has got a wonderful healing power. It is *a panacea* for all ailments.

Sohan:—Sir, what is that magic dose you speak so highly of? May I know it?

Teacher:—Oh, it is a simple and most effective dose, and that is, *"Trust in God and do the Right"*. Your case is very much similar to that of a merchant.

Sohan:—Who was the merchant and what was his problem, Sir?

Teacher:—A merchant was returning home from a fair with a large sum of money which he earned there. He passed through a forest. There was a sudden and heavy downpour of rain. He was put to great suffering as he was forced to spend a cold and rainy night in the forest. He grumbled and blamed God. At day-break, an armed robber sighted him and tried to shoot him, to get possession of his money, but failed, for the powder was damp. The merchant escaped. What saved the merchant from death, my boy?

Sohan:—Yes, Sir, the heavy downpour of rain made the powder damp and proved to be a blessing in disguise which the merchant realised later on.

Teacher:—So, now you understand the mystery. Failure is a better teacher than success, my dear. Henceforward, have full faith in God. Do your duty as best as you can, but leave the rest (success or failure) to the Divine Will. In the Gita, our holy Scripture, the Lord says: "Thy duty is to work, but let not the fruit of action be thy motive."

I shall clear this point by citing to you another incident.

"Once Arjuna and the Lord Krishna went to see a rich man. He was very proud and arrogant. He did not care to receive them, to give them food or any kind of good treatment. He was extremely indifferent.

The Lord Krishna blessed him and said, "Let him get five crores of rupees." Then they went to see a poor pious old man. He had a cow. He worshipped Arjuna and the Lord Krishna and gave them all the milk. The Lord said: "Let his cow die."

Arjuna was extremely surprised and said, "O Lord! I cannot understand your nature. You blessed the rich man who insulted you and cursed the poor man who served you."

The Lord replied: "The rich man will do great crimes through his wealth and will directly go to hell. The poor man will give up the attachment to his cow and come to My abode quickly."

Arjuna said: "My Lord, Thy ways are mysterious. I now understand Thy real nature."

So you see, boys, God knows what is best for us. He does what is best for us. He does what is best suited to our ultimate good. His ways are mysterious. Know His Divine ways and become wise. Face every difficulty and meet the battle of life with a smile, patiently and heroically. Troubles and difficulties come to you to intensify your faith in God, to strengthen your will and power of endurance and turn your mind more and more towards God. Pain is a great eye-opener. Kunti prayed: "O Lord Krishna, give me pain always, so that I may ever remember you." So you realise, God does everything for our own good. Let not little things annoy you. Let not great gains throw you off the balance. Be always calm, balanced and serene. Everything happens as God wills. Pain and sorrow, difficulties and failures are the gifts of God for our purification. So we must resign ourselves to His Will. Surrender yourself to the Lord and do not grumble if you get into difficulties and troubles. Wise men receive with calmness whatever comes their way, good or evil. They neither welcome the one with joy, nor curse the other.

Even so, we should bow down to and accept with equal grace whatever comes, good or evil, believing that it has been ordained by the Beloved Lord for our well-being. We should consider ourselves so many instruments through which God is working out His Divine Will.

Sohan:—Sir, when we work hard, we do so to gain something. Why should we not then, expect the result of our action according to our desire and hard work?

Teacher:—Well asked, my boy. Suppose you want to

join your sister's marriage and apply for a week's leave. Now it depends entirely on the goodwill of your officer to grant you leave. Suppose he says: "No, I am short of hands at this time, I can't spare you and grant your request," what will you do then? Will you curse your officer or resign the post? Will you feel unhappy because you failed to get leave? Can you force him or assert your right for leave, due to you?

Sohan:—No Sir, how can I resign my job? I shall gain nothing by cursing the officer either, if he does not grant me leave. By asserting my rights, I am afraid I would be displeasing him all the more.

Teacher:—Very good. Then it is better for you to resign yourself to your officer's will. If you get leave as you wish, so far so good; don't feel overjoyed at your success. If not, you need not worry. Even so, duties should be performed with firm faith and devotion to God— "Duty for duty's sake"—their fruits or results being offered to the Lord.

Our mind is tossed and agitated not by the work itself but by something else. And it is our desire for the results of our action. That alone makes our mind restless. The non-fulfilment of our desires makes us unhappy. If we stop to seek the fruit of our action, no amount of success or failure can jeopardise our mind.

A GUILTY CONSCIENCE DREADS ITS OWN SHADOW

Teacher:—How have you done your papers in the examination, Gopal?

Gopal:—I have done my papers to my entire satisfaction. The English paper is rather stiff, but I have answered all the questions. I have done ten questions out of ten, all quite right, in mathematics. In Hindi I am sure to secure 75% of the marks. On the whole, I expect a first class in the examination, and God willing, I might secure a scholarship. Our teacher who accompanies us to the examination hall, is very hopeful of my bright result.

Teacher:—Very nice. So, when the results are declared, will you invite all your friends to a grand feast?

Gopal:—Certainly, Sir. I shall welcome all my teachers and classmates to a picnic.

Teacher:—An excellent idea, my boy.

Krishna:—The day before yesterday, a very disheartening incident took place in the examination hall. You will be simply sorry to know about it, Sir.

Teacher:—Has any candidate been turned out of the hall?

Krishna:—Yes, Sir. It happened like this. A boy had brought a few loose papers with him containing answers to certain important questions which he expected in the question-paper that morning. He was busy in copying the answers from the loose papers he had hidden under the desk. All of a sudden, the Superintendent announced that no candidate should keep any loose paper on or under the desk. The candidate concerned, got terribly nervous, thinking that the Superintendent had seen him in the act of copying. So he hurriedly folded the papers to put them in his pocket. The assistant supervisor who was standing a few paces behind the candidate, noticed him and caught him red-handed. He was, immediately, turned out of the examination hall.

Teacher:—What a hard lot! My dear. Can you tell what sort of conscience he possessed? Raise hands those who know.

Krishna:—Yes, Sir, I know, but the word slips off my memory. Just a minute, please, and I shall tell you the exact word. (*Thinks deeply for a minute and then speaks out*). He possessed a *guilty conscience*. Am I correct. Sir?

Teacher:—Quite right, my boy. So you know the proverb, *A guilty conscience dreads its own shadow.*

I want you all to understand things aright. These days, boys don't want to work hard. They want easy and short-cuts to success and would stoop down to employing all possible foul means to achieve it. It is altogether a bad mental attitude. Bear in mind, boys, "Success gained by using unfair means is no success at all." Mahatma Gandhi said, "It is better to forego our goal or object than to achieve it by impure and unfair means. If you want to have success in any undertaking or walk of life, the means you adopt to get it, must also be pure, and not foul. Then alone can you claim to have achieved real success, worth the merit. Similarly, wealth acquired by dishonest means will surely involve us in some trouble or other, but the same obtained by honest and fair means can bring us happiness and good luck."

All such incidents must be eye-openers for you all. I shall just illustrate the aforesaid proverb by giving you a nice funny story.

A rich Brahmin had many servants. One day his silver-pot was stolen. He suspected his servants to have done it, but could not find out the culprit. At last he hit upon a plan. He sent for all his servants. He gave one stick to each and said: "All these sticks are equal. Each stick is one yard long. But, by tomorrow morning, the stick of the thief shall grow one inch longer than those of others."

All went back to their places. At night the thief thought to himself, "The master is a very wise man. As I have stolen the pot, my stick will grow one inch longer and I shall be found out. It is better if I cut one inch off my stick." So he took his stick and cut off one inch. The next morning the master called them again to show their sticks. He saw that one stick was shorter than the other sticks by one inch. So the owner of that stick was caught as the thief. The Brahmin got his silver-pot back and the guilty servant was dismissed.

Gopal:—Sir, may I tell a similar incident of a guilty conscience?

Teacher:—Yes. All will welcome it.

Gopal:—Once there was a rich cotton-merchant in a town. He kept a large stock of cotton. One night some thieves stole away a heap of cotton. He tried his best to find out the thieves, but he got no clue.

An old man said to the merchant: "Give a feast to your people and I shall catch the thieves." The merchant agreed to it. When the guests were enjoying the feast, the old man shouted: "Cotton is still sticking to the beards of the thieves!" At this the guilty men unconsciously put their hands to their beards to remove it. They were thus caught in the trap.

Teacher:—Very good. It is also a very instructive story illustrating the same truth. A man possessing a guilty conscience can never succeed or prosper in life. He can't be bold, honest and straightforward.

Have you noticed, boys, some passengers travel by train, without tickets, though they know very well that they will be charged almost double the railway fare with penalty, if they are detected? Only experienced persons can realise the wretched mental condition of the passenger travelling without ticket. He feels terribly uneasy. He has to be constantly on the alert. He keeps his head out of the window to watch the movements of the T.T.E. from compartment to compartment in the running train.

Because of his guilty conscience, he suffers from constant dread of being detected and penalised. If the T.T.E. happens to enter his compartment, he hides himself in the lavatory to avoid and escape from his searching eye. After passing some time there, he comes out, and, to his utter disappointment and surprise, finds the T.T.E. still in the compartment. He is asked to produce his ticket. The wretched person looks blank and pays the necessary fare with penalty.

So, my boys, never avoid payment of your dues, whatever they may be; have a clear conscience, and be fearless and bold.

MUTUAL HELP AND CO-OPERATION LEAD TO HAPPINESS

Teacher:—What was all that singing and noise about on the loudspeaker last night, Vikram? It disturbed me a lot.

Vikram:—There was a marriage-celebration in my neighbourhood, Sir.

Teacher:—Oh! So you enjoyed the marriage-festivities last night. (Laughing) I am reminded of the man who became bankrupt in celebrating his daughter's marriage.

Vikram:—Who was the man, and how it all happened, Sir?

Teacher:—A man had four sons. They quarrelled amongst themselves. He tried his best to make them live in peace but in vain. After a few years the father died. The sons still continued to quarrel on trifles, and their differences multiplied from day to day. Each earned his own living, quite independent of the others.

A few years later, one of the daughters of the eldest brother came of marriageable age. The date of marriage was fixed. Narendra, the eldest brother was in a fix as to how to make arrangements for the various ceremonies, single-handed. He never expected any help or co-operation from his brothers because of their age-long indifference towards one another. He thought and thought over the matter and hit upon a plan. He invited his so-called fast friends and discussed the whole marriage-affair with them. The friends were well aware of his strained relations with his brothers and took the best advantage of the situation. They said: "My dear friend, why do you worry? It is a simple affair. Let your brothers go to dogs; we shall arrange everything. We will chalk out the whole programme of marriage and will put up the best show possible." Narendra had to trust the sincerity of his fair-weather friends. A rough estimate of the expenditure was made, and money was advanced to them for the purchase of necessary articles—provisions, sweets, fruits, ornaments, clothes, and other items, including the entertainment of the bridegroom's party, feasting, dance, and music, refreshments, etc., etc.

The marriage was over. The whole function extended over two or three days. Now, boys, you can very well guess the result. The goldsmith, the cloth-merchant, the sweetmeat-seller and other petty shop-keepers submitted their respective bills. The expenditure far exceeded the estimate by double the amount; poor Narendra became bankrupt and felt extremely unhappy and miserable.

What was all this trouble due to, you know?

Krishna:—Yes, Sir, Narendra's so-called fast friends played him false, cheated him and enjoyed at his cost.

Vikram:—Sir, they were real brothers after all. How and why could they not co-operate with and help Narendra on that important occasion of his daughter's marriage?

Teacher:—They badly lacked in adaptability, my boy. Egoism and pride were two serious obstacles in their way of developing adaptability.

Krishna.—What do you mean by adaptability, Sir?

Teacher:—Adaptability is a virtue or noble quality by which one adapts or fits oneself with others, whatever their nature or temperaments may be. This is a most desirable habit or quality for success in life. This virtue must be developed slowly. The vast majority of persons do not know how to adjust or fit themselves with others.

Krishna:—What are the attributes of a man of adaptability, Sir?

Teacher:—Very good. It is an intelligent question. A man of adaptability or accommodating nature has to make some sacrifice. For example, if a clerk understands well the ways, habits and temperament of his superior and accordingly, adjusts himself nicely to suit his ways, his superior becomes a slave of the clerk. A few kind words to soften the superior's heart are all that is needed. Speak gently and sweetly. Carry out his orders to the very letter, because the officer wants a little respect. It costs you nothing. Then your superior will have a soft corner for you in his heart. He will do whatever you want. He will overlook your mistakes. You become his pet. Humility and obedience are necessary for developing adaptability. A proud egoistic man finds it very difficult to adapt himself. So he is always in trouble.

A man of adaptability has to share with others what he has. Sometimes he has to bear insult and harsh words. He has to develop patience, endurance and balance of mind. These virtues develop by themselves, when he tries to adapt himself with others.

Gopal:—Now I understand, Sir, why Narendra, who celebrated his daughter's marriage, came to trouble. Each was too proud to fit himself with his other brothers. They differed with one another in their temperaments and none tried or cared to adapt himself with the other. Hence mutual help and co-operation was out of question.

Teacher:—Exactly so. Can you tell me any other story illustrative of mutual help and co-operation?

Gopal:—Yes, Sir, why not?

Once two sheep were passing over a narrow bridge. They were coming from opposite directions. They met in the middle of the bridge. The bridge was only a log of wood. They could not turn back.

One sheep said: "I am very sorry. I did not notice you coming. What shoud we do now? We cannot go back."

The other said: "You are not to blame. I also did not see you. It is my fault. I shall jump into the water, and then you may pass on."

The first shouted: "No, do not do that; you will certainly be drowned, because the water is very deep and the current is strong. I shall lie down and you pass over my body gently."

So the first sheep lay down flat and the other passed over its body very gently. In this way both of them were able to cross the bridge. They thanked and bade each other good-bye.

Teacher:—Excellent. You told a very nice story which clearly illustrates: *"Mutual help and co-operation lead to happiness."* So, boys, ADAPT, ADJUST, ACCOMMODATE, and you will have all success in life. May God bless you.

Boys:—Thank you very much, Sir.

OUT OF GOOD LIFE COMES GOD-LIFE

Teacher:—Well, boys, you have been listening to a number of moral and spiritual talks for the last so many days. I am going to put a few questions, this morning, to see if you can give satisfactory answers.

Mohan, why is it good to help a man who is in trouble or in difficulties?

Mohan:—Because it will refine and ennoble our character, Sir, and because the same Lord is in him also. Service of man is service of God. Practice of charitable acts, compassion, kind service and little acts of sacrifice purify, expand and soften our heart and prepare us for the reception of Divine Light.

Teacher:—Excellent! Your answer is short and sweet, and to my entire satisfaction. But can you define or explain what you mean by *acts of sacrifice?*

Mohan:—Sir, I find it a bit difficult to define, but I can give you a clear idea of what I mean by an act of sacrifice, by quoting an incident to which I was an eye-witness.

Teacher:—Yes, by all means. You are quite welcome with your description of the incident.

Mohan:—A fire broke out yesterday in a two-storeyed house. The mistress of the house, after preparing the evening meal retired to her sleeping chamber, along with her children. The master of the house was not at home. By accident a piece of cloth which was lying near the fire-place caught fire. The fire spread to a heap of wood which was lying close by and the whole house was on fire. The mistress of the house, thinking that all was safe, bolted the door from inside and fell into sleep. The flames rose, and rose, and the whole street was up. There gathered a crowd of people. They called the master of the house, but none gave any reply. Hearing a great noise outside, the mistress awoke and was horrified to find her house full of smoke and flames. She awoke her children, and in bewilderment took them to the roof. She began to cry aloud piteously for help. The people tried to put out the fire with pitchers and buckets full of water, but all was in vain. Nobody cared to listen to her heart-rending cries and wailings. But a young neighbour applied a wooden ladder against the wall and leapt on the roof and, in a few minutes, brought down the woman and children safe and sound.

Soon after, the fire-brigade arrived and began to work. It took two full hours to extinguish the fire. All the furniture was reduced to ashes. By the grace of God, there was no loss of life.

The mistress shed tears of delight, took off her diamond ring, and offered it to the saviour of her children, as a reward. He thanked her for the gift, but returned it to her, saying, "We scouts do not accept any reward for our service. I have done my duty, nothing more."

Everybody admired the courage and selfless service of the scout who had saved the mistress and her children at the risk of his own life.

Teacher: Very good, my boy. One who saves others, at the risk of his own life, is a true hero, and such an act of selfless service is called an act of sacrifice. Some other people from amidst the crowd, also, did their bit of selfless service trying to put out the fire with pitchers and buckets of water, but that help was small in comparison with the courage and gallant service done by the scout.

And what was still more wonderful on his part? Did you notice it, boys?

Gopal:—Yes, Sir, the most creditable and praiseworthy feature was that he did not accept the lady's offer of the diamond ring as a reward. He performed duty for duty's sake. He was a real Karma Yogin.

Teacher:—Right you are, my dear. A good deed is never lost. It purifies the heart and leads to the dawn of Divine Grace and Divine Light. Goodness makes life a blessing and brings sure success and prosperity.

Feeding the hungry, nursing the sick, clothing the naked, helping the poor and needy with money, and sharing what you have with others, without a thought of getting any return or reward from them, are all little acts of selfless service and sacrifice. You should not lose any opportunity, and do these charitable acts daily, and realise the benefits yourself. Let your life be a living expression of love, sacrifice, wisdom and courage.

Can you tell me, Krishna, why is it bad to injure or kill any being?

Krishna:—Because the end is unworthy. It will reduce us to the level of a brute. If we injure another life, we do but injure our own life; and if we help another, we do but help our own self. There is but one life (Atman), one God, in all beings.

Teacher: Wonderful! Your answer is as good and to the point as that of Mohan. I am pleased to find that you have been benefited much by our daily talks.

Krishna:—May I tell another story, Sir, illustrating the truth: "*Self-sacrifice is always honoured*"?

Teacher:—Yes, you can, but in five minutes' time.

Krishna:—Once there was a Rajput nurse in the service of the Rana of Jodhpur. Her name was Moti. The mother of the only prince had died; so he was put in charge of the faithful nurse. One day a party of the Rana's enemies came into the palace. They were seeking to kill the prince. Moti at once dressed her own son in the clothes of the prince and put him in his place.

The cruel enemies put the child to the sword. She saw her son being slain but she did not cry. Thus she saved the life of her master's son, the prince, at the cost of her own son. She will ever be remembered as an example of bravery, loyalty and self-sacrifice.

Teacher:—Very nice. It is a simple, short story. She set an example of the noblest self-sacrifice ever performed by a lady.

AN EVIL ACTION RECOILS ON THE HEAD OF THE EVIL-DOER

Teacher:—Hello, master Vikram! Can you tell me the most important moral that you have learnt from our talks?

Vikram:—You take me unawares, Sir. I have not revised the topic in my mind. If you allow me two minutes, I can tell you everything.

Teacher:—All right. Go on with your mental revision.

Vikram:—Yes, now I recollect, Sir. *"Do unto others as you wish to be done by." "Love begets love, hatred begets hatred."* Am I right Sir?

Teacher:—Quite correct. Your memory is very sharp. Is there any other lesson left out?

Vijaya:—Yes, Sir. "We should return good for

evil,—the Golden Rule." We should not retaliate, but should be large-hearted and charitable.

Teacher:—Very nice. If you keep all these ideals before you and practise these virtues, you will have quick success, and most of your problems in life will be solved. You know, my dear, "Life without virtuous qualities is like a desert without oases." So let your life be a living expression of unselfish love, sacrifice, wisdom and goodwill. If you give respect and sympathy to others, you will receive respect and sympathy in return.

Vijaya, can you name any two instructions out of so many you have received so far?

Vijaya:—Yes Sir, "We should practise non-injury." We should think twice before we act, because "haste makes waste."

Teacher:—Excellent. You know, my dear, wounding the feeling of others even by gesture, expression, tone of voice or unkind words is also injury. Righteousness is the Divine path. Wealth, beauty, honour and youth fade away, but a life of righteousness will never decay.

Mohan:—Sir, are you not going to take up any story this morning, as usual?

Teacher:—Oh yes, that will surely come, but it is good to assimilate what you have got so far.

All right, who comes forward with a nice, short but funny story, this morning?

Sohan:—(begins) Once there were three wicked men. They used to go out together in search of loot. They divided amongst themselves equally whatever they got in this way. One day they found a big stone under a tree.

They thought that there would be some treasure underneath that stone. So they removed the stone and found a pit.

They dug out the pit and found an iron-safe. They broke open the seal. To their great delight, it was full of gold and silver coins. But it was too heavy to be carried away. They sent one man to fetch a cart. When he left, the other two companions began to talk. One of them said to the other, "Will it not be much better if we two can share the whole treasure? We two can easily do away with the third when he returns. Then each of us will have half the treasure instead of one-third." The other man was of the same opinion. They devised a plan to murder their third companion immediately on his arrival.

The third man reached the town, hired a cart and bought some wine and sweets. He too was as wicked as his two associates. He thought to himself, "If I could get the whole of the treasure, I would be able to live in peace for the rest of my life." Thinking this, he put some poison into the wine.

As soon as he reached the jungle, his two friends fell upon him and put him to death, before he could utter a word. They were so very pleased at their easy success that they began to eat sweets and drink wine before putting the iron-safe on the cart. The next moment, they, too, fell dead on the ground beside the open pit, and the treasure remained where it was.

Vijaya:—O, what a tragedy! I really pity their lot. Usually they must have been sharing among themselves equally whatever they got by loot. But this time what happened to them, so that each thought of getting the whole treasure for himself? I fail to understand this sort of mentality. What made them think like that, Sir?

Teacher:—Yes, my dear, they were all birds of the same feather. This time they were overpowered with greed that brought their total destruction. *Greed or craving for wealth is a great evil.* Greed clouds the intellect or understanding and makes a man absolutely blind. It obscures the mind. Greed makes the mind restless. It is insatiable. There is no end to it. A greedy man is extremely selfish; he looks to his own interests and cares not a bit for others.

What are the three gates to hell? Do you remember, Ajay?

Ajay:—Lust, Anger and Greed, Sir.

Teacher:—Very good. Greed is one of them. So, now, you see, boys, how this great evil, greed, works havoc when it overpowers a man. Do you know its antidote? What is the best way to conquer this dreadful evil?

Mohan:—Yes, Sir. You explained to us the other day that one can conquer such evils by developing opposite and positive virtues.

Teacher:— Exactly so. You are perfectly right. So you see, contentment is the supreme wealth. It cools the fire of greed. The positive always overcomes the negative. This is the law of Nature. Negative, evil thoughts cannot stand before positive good thoughts. For example, courage overcomes fear, just as light overcomes or removes darkness. Patience overcomes anger. Even so, generosity or contentment overcomes greed, and so on.

Sohan:—Yes, Sir. Now I understand. If each of the wicked men had felt contented with one-third of his share of the treasure, this tragedy of utter ruin or destruction could have been avoided. They would have escaped that terrible fate. But greed made them blind, and each thought of enriching himself alone by getting the whole of the treasure. What a pity!

Teacher:—Remember, boys: "If you dig a pit for others, you yourself will fall into it." There is a close relationship between greed and Moha (attachment). A greedy man has got great Moha for his money. His mind is always on the money-box and the bunch of keys he has tied to his waist-cord. Money is his very blood and life. He lives to collect money. He is only a gate-keeper to his money, so to say. The enjoyer is his prodigal son.

Money-lenders always fall victims to this evil of greed. They suck the blood of poor people by taking enormous interest, 25 per cent and even 50 per cent at times. They pretend to show that they are of charitable disposition by doing acts, such as opening of Kshetras, building temples, etc. These things cannot wash off the sins of merciless acts. Many poor families are ruined by these cruel-hearted people. A man with one lakh of rupees plans to get ten lakhs. A millionaire schemes to become a multi-millionaire. There is no end to their greed.

Like charity, greed also takes up various forms. A man thirsts for name and fame and applause. This is greed. A sub-judge thirsts for becoming a High Court judge. A third-class magistrate thirsts for becoming a first-class magistrate with full powers. This is also greed.

Do you know the story of "The goose that laid golden eggs?"

Vijaya:—Yes, Sir. May I tell the story in brief? My friends may be curious to know it. A farmer had a wonderful goose which laid an egg of pure gold every day. As he grew very rich he became all the more greedy. He was impatient and could not bear to have only one egg a day. Hoping to get all the eggs at once, the foolish farmer killed the goose, and began to search the body of the dead goose for gold. But he could find nothing. Then he tore his hair and cursed himself for his foolishness. He repented very much for the loss of the goose; but all his sorrow and grief was in vain.

Teacher:—Very good. It is a nice, short and instructive story. It teaches us: "A man should not be greedy lest he should lose what he already has."

Who was Midas? Do you know, Sohan?

Sohan:— No, Sir.

Teacher:—Then, listen to this story. It is something very interesting.

Midas was a king. He was very greedy. He asked for a boon that everything he touched might turn into gold. The boon was granted. He touched all trees in his garden and they turned into gold. He became very happy. When he sat down to eat and touched his food, it also turned into hot morsels of gold. The poor man could not satisfy his hunger as his mouth and tongue were burnt up. And what was still worse, his daughter jumped into his lap, and was instantaneously turned into a lifeless statue of gold. Now, the king became most unhappy. He began to curse

himself for his stupidity. He then prayed for the cancel-
lation of the boon which was granted.

So, my dear, don't be greedy. Share with others what
you have. Do not cause pain or suffering to any living
being through greed, selfishness or ill-will. Give up the
spirit of fighting, and heated debates. Do not argue. If
you quarrel with somebody or if you have a heated argument with anybody, your balance of mind will be upset.
Much energy will be wasted in useless channels. The
blood will become hot. The nerves will be shattered. You
must try your level best to keep a serene mind always.

Teacher:—Now, my boys, I am afraid we are getting
late for lunch. We meet again tomorrow. I wish you all
good luck.

Boys:—Thank you very much, Sir.

APPENDIX

RIDDLES

1. How high can an elephant jump?
2. What is that which bites without mouth and teeth?
3. What is that which makes Adam a woman?
4. Wherefrom can a dog get its tail, if it loses it?
5. What is that which is more useful when broken?
6. He hears without ears, sees without eyes, tastes without tongue. Who is he?
7. What is it that you can swallow but can swallow you, too?
8. I have cities, but no houses; forests, but no trees; rivers, but no water. What am I?
9. What do you throw out when you need it, and take in when you don't?
10. I am something that always increases the more I am shared with others, What am I?
11. Why is the letter G very sweet?
12. What has bed but never sleeps?
13. What goes up a hill and down a hill, but never moves?
14. How many lines has a Gramophone record got?
15. What is the difference between a school-master and an engine-driver?
16. What has holes but still can carry water?
17. What has a head and foot but cannot think or walk?
18. What has a thousand needles but cannot sew?
19. What is taken from you before you get it?

20. What has eyes but cannot see?
21. What goes round the world yet stays in one corner?
22. What goes through the window without breaking it?
23. Can a leopard change its spot?
24. A is the father of B; but B is not the son of A What then?
25. What is that you cannot see, but is always before you?
26. Who handles more letters than a postman?
27. What is it that won't cry out if you strike it?
28. To what question may you never answer 'yes'?
29. What is that which increases when it is shared with others?
30. Who is the man that does not do a day's work but still gets his pay?

ANSWERS

1. The elephant cannot jump.
2. Shoes.
3. Add 'M'......(Madam).
4. From a Re-tail shop.
5. 'Coconut in Malabar, and 'Egg' in London.
6 *Brahman.*
7. Water.
8. Map.
9. Anchor.
10. Knowledge.
11. Because it is in the middle of *Sugar.*
12. River.
13. Road.
14. One line.
15. The school-master trains the mind and the engine driver minds the train.

16. Sponge.
17. A hill.
18. Porcupine.
19. Photo or picture or portrait.
20. Potato or pine-apple.
21. Stamp.
22. Light.
23. Yes, When it goes from one spot to another.
24. Daughter.
25. Your future.
26. A type-setter.
27. A match.
28. Are you asleep?
29. Happiness.
30. A night-watcher.